Delegate for Results

How to Accomplish More Through Others

Compliments of
RUCEC Onsite Training
800-344-4613

Edited by National Press Publications

NATIONAL PRESS PUBLICATIONS

A Division of Rockhurst University Continuing Education Center, Inc.
6901 West 63rd Street • P.O. Box 2949 • Shawnee Mission, Kansas 66201-1349
1-800-258-7248 • 1-913-432-7757

National Press Publications endorses nonsexist language. In an effort to make this handbook clear, consistent and easy to read, we have used "he" throughout the odd-numbered chapters and "she" throughout the even-numbered chapters. The copy is not intended to be sexist.

Delegate for Results: How to Accomplish More Through Others

Published by National Press Publications, Inc.
Copyright 2000, National Press Publications, Inc.
A Division of Rockhurst University Continuing Education Center, Inc.

Printed in the United States of America

6 7 8 9 10

ISBN 1-55852-276-x

Table of Contents

Introduction v

1 Delegation: an Overview...1
   What Delegation Is … and Isn't...1
   Delegation "Musts" 2
   Steps to Effective Delegation 5

2 The Advantages of Delegation....................................9
   Benefits of Effective Delegation for the Manager 9
   Benefits of Effective Delegation for Subordinates 10
   Benefits of Effective Delegation to the Organization 11
   Consequences of the Failure to Delegate 13

3 Barriers to Delegation...19
   Barriers in the Manager...19
   Barriers in the Subordinate..21
   Barriers in the Situation..22

4 What to Delegate 25

5 What Not to Delegate 31

6 Planning What to Delegate 37
   Step 1: Analyze and Assess Your Job..................................37
   Step 2: Analyze and Assess Your Subordinates 38
   Work Style Profile...39

7 Effective Goal-Setting in the Delegation Process 43
   The Role of Expectations and Goals...................................43
   Matching the Goal and the Delegatee 46

8 Choosing a Delegatee..49
   Assessing the Personalities of Potential Delegatees 52

9 Developing People Power Through Delegation 57
   What Motivates Employees...58
   Communication 62

10 The Delegation Conference..**69**
Why a Delegation Conference?...69
The Steps in the Delegation Process 70

11 Letting Go...**77**
"Stewardship" Delegation 77

12 Responsibility...**85**
Ten Tips When Employee Accountability Is Lacking 86

13 The Importance of Spot-Checking Delegation **91**
Case Study 91
Tools for Delegation 92

14 Making It Stick — Handling Reverse Delegation...............................**99**
Ways to Empower and Motivate 101

15 Handling Projects Delegated to You **105**

Index **109**

INTRODUCTION

Knowing how much to delegate is a difficult problem for managers. Somewhere along the way, the successful manager learns to switch the focus of activity from doing to planning. There is a direct correlation between management position and the amount of time required in planning and in operating. The allocation of time to managerial functions such as planning is not fixed. It varies from industry to industry and from one person to another.

Susan and Marge went to work at a local bank directly after graduating from high school. They entered as clerk/typists. They "learned the ropes" and worked hard. Each began to advance from clerk to secretary to teller to account representative. These young women were go-getters. They knew the business better than other clerk/typists. They were good, and they knew it. They thrived on challenge and learning.

As they moved up their professional ladders, they moved into positions of greater supervisory importance. In the span of a few years, each was promoted to assistant vice president of the bank. No one doubted that Susan was capable. Over the years, Susan had acquired a talent for handling the bank's computer programming problems. She worked hard, was thorough and was capable of meeting demands. Yet Marge was obviously "star" material. Somehow Marge seemed a step ahead of Susan.

Susan's people always delivered their workload in a capable manner, but that was it. They did the job and nothing more. What happened to Susan? Somewhere along the way, Susan was sidetracked. She missed the "switch." Because of her history of hard work with the organization, she found it difficult to overcome her superwoman mentality. She was unable to settle for less than what she considered perfect. Susan was a "doer," not a "delegator." Marge stayed on track and made the "switch" from doer to delegator.

The higher you advance up the managerial ladder, the less time you should spend "doing" specific tasks. The higher you advance, the more time you should spend planning and managing. Saxon Tate, managing director of Canada and Dominion Sugar, explains this process by saying:

"Decisions simply must be made at the lowest possible level
for management at the top to maintain its effectiveness. I make
few decisions with a time span of less than a year. At one point,
I made them for as short a time span as one week. I now see that
kind of involvement in detail as a luxury no man at the top can afford."

Robert H. Breckenridge, president and chief executive officer of the fast-growing Vitronics Corporation, recalls once taking over a new job and being told by his boss "to make sure you are the least busy of all the people associated with you." Says Breckenridge:

"By this he meant that I should organize myself and the
people who worked for me so that I had the least to do
on a day-to-day basis, and could spend time thinking
about the actual future of the business."

The Pareto Principle observes that 80 percent of the work is done by 20 percent of the people. Have you experienced days when you felt that 99 percent of the work was done by 1 percent of the people — namely you? By failing to delegate, you are leading an army of one … and armies of one go nowhere. A great coach doesn't don the helmet and shoulder pads and go out on the field to block and tackle. He concentrates on strategy and tactics. The most effective managers are more concept-oriented than task-oriented.

Planning is exerting control over the future. You cannot control the future if you are trapped in the present. For those trapped in the present, a key to the future is delegation. Delegation is assigning to others specific tasks and the requisite authority to complete those tasks, with mutually agreed-upon methods for evaluating the completed work. The primary reason that managers fail is that they fail to delegate properly. Delegation is a leveraging technique.

The successful delegator can double or triple his or her productivity. The nondelegator works frantically, grabs lunches, lugs briefcases, is subjective and generally ineffective. The delegator has time for work and a personal life, works effectively and views life objectively. The advantages of delegation are quite simple — you are using other people's brains for your gains.

A top investment banker recently attended a time-management seminar. Accurately assessing his delegation problems, he returned to the office determined to make changes. He and his secretary listed every item that had crossed his desk in the last week — phone calls, memos, requests for reports, etc. He noted the relative importance of every item, whether it could have been delegated and, if so, to whom. He then directed all assignable tasks to the appropriate persons with instructions "to handle the tasks."

This executive described the reaction as follows: "Some dust was stirred up. There were a lot of discussions, but almost every single delegated task was effectively handled. Many of them were taken care of far better than if I had done them. This changed my whole outlook on the job and has made me far more effective."

As the axiom goes, you learn to work smarter, not harder. The choice is yours. Are you ready to make the switch?

Steps to Working Smarter, Not Harder

1. Be effective rather than efficient. Focus on the most important tasks at hand.

2. Establish a set of goals, objectives and time frames for achievement.

3. Prioritize. Make the hard choices.

4. Analyze your current use of time, energy and resources.

5. Realign your use of time, energy and resources to match your priorities.

6. Delegate what you don't do well, what someone else can do better or what is a lower priority item.

7. Eliminate (not reduce — eliminate) nonessentials and clutter to maximize the effectiveness of your work/living space … and time.

8. Find your peak productivity time and factor that knowledge into your daily planning.

9. Continually reassess and adjust. Life/work is dynamic and ever-changing. So must be your approach to it.

10. Take a walk. Clear your head periodically … and smell the roses.

1 DELEGATION: AN OVERVIEW

"The surest way for an executive to kill himself is to refuse to learn how, and when, and to whom to delegate work."

— J.C. Penney

Managers frequently complain that they have too much to do and too little time in which to do it. Unchecked, this feeling leads to stress and managerial ineffectiveness. In many cases, managers could greatly reduce their stress by practicing the critical management skill of delegation. The inability to delegate has led to the downfall of many leaders — from presidents to first-line supervisors.

So exactly what is delegation? And why does it take an entire handbook to explain it? Isn't it just handing off a task to someone else? Hardly. This chapter will examine what delegation is and isn't, and provide an overview of the steps of an effective delegation process.

What Delegation Is ... and Isn't

Delegation is not task assignment. Task assignment is simply assigning work to an individual within the duties and responsibilities of his position.

Delegation is not "dumping." You should take special care to be sure the employee does not think you are "dumping" unpleasant assignments on him. If delegation is handled improperly, the employee feels resentful about doing part of the boss's work.

Delegation is not abdication. The manager still has the ultimate accountability for the assignment. That's why it is important for you to establish appropriate controls and checkpoints to monitor progress.

Delegation is a tool to align duties for **maximum results** while avoiding overload and burnout.

Delegation involves the manager giving someone the responsibility, authority and accountability to do something that is normally part of the manager's job.

- **Responsibility** refers to the assignment itself and the intended results. That means setting clear expectations … and avoiding the urge to dictate *how* the assignment should be completed.

- **Authority** refers to the appropriate power given to the individual or group, including the right to act and make decisions. This is critical if the delegatee is to complete the job successfully. It's very important to communicate boundaries, limitations and criteria such as budgetary considerations.

- **Accountability** refers to the fact that the individual must "answer" for his actions and decisions … receiving the rewards or penalties that accompany those actions or decisions.

Delegation "Musts"

- **Understand the need for delegation.** The manager must understand and agree that delegation is necessary. Subordinates must understand their obligations.

- **Designate goals and objectives.** Organizational goals and objectives must be clearly understood by all parties, and there should be general agreement on what is to be done when, how, why, how well, in what priority, with what resources and by whom.

- **Know strengths — and weaknesses — of subordinates.** In order for the supervisor to delegate according to individual capabilities and interests, he must know the characteristics and talents of each individual.

- **Communicate with superiors.** The supervisor should reach agreement with his manager(s) about what is to be delegated and what the supervisor is expected to do personally.

- **Establish performance standards.** Performance standards must encourage individual initiative, creativity and organizational loyalty. The delegator and the subordinate should agree on exactly what the standards are … preferably with the subordinate actively participating in their creation.

- **Agree on exceptions.** Any deviation should be clearly explained by the supervisor and should be understood to be an exception rather than the rule.

- **Plan for determining skills and training.** Delegation should include the opportunity for testing employees' skills and for providing any necessary assistance.

- **Show your interest.** The supervisor should show genuine interest in what is being done by the subordinates.

- **Measure results.** Assessments can be done in a variety of ways. Use various systems to report in key areas, measure performance and evaluate standards of achievement.

- **Offer help and additional training.** Continuous training can bring about self-corrections by subordinates.

Personal Attributes of a Successful Delegator

- **Has charisma and respect**

  Sees things from numerous perspectives. Conveys dedication and a strong sense of mission. Honors the opinions and work of others, irrespective of their status or position.

- **Stimulates creativity**

  Communicates in ways that force others to rethink ideas that they had never questioned before. Sparks flow free of thought.

- **Gives individual consideration**

  Actively listens and supports. Coaches and advises as needed.

- **Displays courage and accountability**

  Will stand up for what's right for the company and for employees even if it is unpopular or politically incorrect and causes personal hardship.

- **Is adaptable and flexible**

  Adjusts easily in fluid situations. Juggles multiple problems with ease. Keeps his cool in times of crisis.

- **Exemplifies integrity and good judgment**

  Is a consistent role model of moral and ethical behavior. Reaches sound and objective conclusions.

Steps to Effective Delegation

Step 1: Looking at your present position

    A. What decision do you make most often?

    B. What duties can someone else do?

    C. In what area(s) do your subordinates need development?

    D. Do you or some of your subordinates need more work variety?

Step 2: Planning the delegation

    A. Delegate a whole project, not just bits and pieces.

    B. Consider all the details and necessary steps for successful completion.

    C. Decide the level of authority needed by the employee to accomplish the project.

    D. Think about how this assignment fits into the overall accomplishment of the organizational goals.

Step 3: Choosing whom to delegate to

    A. What are the interests and abilities of your members?

    B. Who needs a challenge? Would this project provide one for this individual?

    C. What is the workload of this individual?

    D. Has anyone expressed interest in the task?

Step 4: Delegation itself

A. Review all the details and necessary steps for successful completion with the individual selected.

B. Detail the specific results you expect to obtain.

C. Decide on a mutually agreeable reporting system during the project's time frame.

D. Explain the level of authority the individual will have while completing the project.

E. Explain how the project fits into the overall accomplishment of the organizational goals.

Step 5: Delegation follow-up

A. Are you allowing the worker the level of authority you agreed upon?

B. Is the project on schedule?

C. Is the reporting system you agreed upon being used?

D. Are you reinforcing the accomplishments of the individual?

E. Are you taking corrective measures when necessary?

F. Are you available for the worker's questions?

G. Remember to say thank you. It's the most neglected form of compensation.

A Short List of Delegation Tips

- Only delegate to people you trust.

- Delegate outcomes; don't dump problems.

- Ask the delegatee to develop milestones, etc., even if you already know what they should be.

- Discuss the consequences of failure. Establish a reporting system designed to catch problems long before they become critical ones.

- Prepare to spend three times as much time with the delegatee as you think you will need.

Rate yourself on each of the following 10 questions using this scale:

Definite Strength	10 - 9
Moderately Effective	8 - 7
Average Performance	6 - 5
Rarely Effective	4 - 3
Definite Weakness	2 - 1

1. Do my subordinates understand our objectives and know what is to be done when, how well and by whom?

2. Do I know which of my responsibilities I must meet myself and which I can delegate?

3. Do I encourage initiative in my subordinates?

4. Do I leave the final decision to subordinates often enough?

5. Do I avoid doing the work of my subordinates?

6. Do I show genuine interest in the work my subordinates are doing?

7. Am I confident that my subordinates can handle the work I give them?

8. Do I give subordinates the guidance, training and authority they need to make decisions independently?

9. Do I regularly assess the quality of my work and that of my subordinates?

10. Do I use delegation to help my subordinates gain new skills and grow in the organization?

Score:	80 - 100	Excellent strength to build upon
	60 - 80	Acceptable ... but could use improvement
	40 - 60	Weak area — better get started on an improvement plan
	under 40	Expect trouble if not improved soon

Reflections

2 THE ADVANTAGES OF DELEGATION

"There are people who want to be everywhere at once and they seem to get nowhere."

— Carl Sandburg

Poor delegation means poor management. Good delegation is the cornerstone of good management skills. Ineffective delegation hinders the success of an entire office. Ineffective delegation drains energy right out of the workplace. Lack of delegation also holds families hostage to never-ending workloads.

Obviously, there are many benefits to effective delegation. This chapter is devoted to outlining those benefits — to the manager, to the employees and to the organization.

Benefits of Effective Delegation for the Manager

- **Makes your job easier.**

- **Allows you to achieve more.** You can achieve greater productivity. Through the proper selection, assignment and coordination of tasks, you can mobilize resources to achieve more than would have been individually possible.

- **Makes you look good.**

- **Allows time for true managerial activities.** Delegation gives you an opportunity to handle aspects of the job that no one else can do. These might include project planning, monitoring team-member performance and handling personnel problems. By using proper delegation, you can focus on doing a few tasks well rather than too many tasks poorly.

- **Increases your promotion potential.** If you don't have the people in the department who are trained to handle responsibilities, you will be chained to one area, and opportunities for promotion will pass you by. Grooming your successor allows you to move on to bigger and better things. Many managers derail their own advancement by not delegating to subordinates and preparing them for advancement to managerial positions.

John Henry Patterson, founder of NCR Company, would walk into his various departments and order the managers to take a two-week vacation. Why? To determine whether a team member had been adequately trained to take over the supervisor's job on short notice. Patterson believed the key to such training was delegation — providing the team member with the experience, knowledge and responsibility needed for a smooth transition.

Benefits of Effective Delegation for Subordinates

- **Team members are more highly motivated with effective delegation.**

- **Delegation develops team members' skills.** It gives your employees a chance to learn and grow … and encourages initiative. Failure to delegate effectively deprives team members of opportunities to improve their skills and assume greater responsibility.

- **Gives employees personal satisfaction and a sense of achievement.**

- **Enhances retention of your most talented team members.** These individuals are the most likely to leave if they are not learning and gaining the experience they should, and they are the ones you can least afford to lose. Using effective delegation, you can keep them from moving on to more challenging and supportive environments.

- **Effective delegation increases team-member involvement.** It encourages employees to understand and influence the work the department does. It allows team members a chance to incorporate their values in the workplace and, in many cases, to work on activities that especially interest them. Increasing team members' involvement in the workplace increases their enthusiasm and initiative.

- **Enhances your employees' value to the organization.** The more skill areas an employee has developed and demonstrated proficiency in, the more valuable she is to the organization. This can provide critical job security during uncertain times.

- **Increases promotion potential.** A team member who receives extensive delegation will be ready and able to advance to new positions. Delegation serves both to train and to test the employee.

- **Increases employee involvement in decision-making.** This, in turn, leads to more commitment and increased morale as well as better decisions.

Benefits of Effective Delegation to the Organization

- **Maximizes efficient output.** When you delegate tasks according to the skills and abilities of each member of the work group, the department as a whole is likely to produce a high level of work. Work also will be completed more efficiently.

- **Makes the best use of available human resources.** In addition, delegation allows new ideas, perspectives and suggestions to flourish.

- **Produces faster, more effective decisions.** An organization is most responsive to change in the environment when decisions are made by those individuals closest to the problems, that is, when responsibility and decision-making are pushed further down the organizational structure.

- **Promotes teamwork.**

- **The organization can be more competitive.** Through delegation, individuals closest to the problem have the most information on which to base an intelligent decision, making decision-making more expedient.

- **Enhances employee commitment to the organization.** When team members participate in decision-making, there is an increase in employee motivation, morale, job performance and commitment to the job and the organization.

- **Saves money.**

- **Increases flexibility of operations.** Effective delegation trains many people to do the same assignments. This overlap allows for greater flexibility of work assignments. When someone is absent or a crisis requires people to assist with tasks not regularly a part of their jobs, they will already be familiar with the assignment. Delegation prepares more individuals for promotion or rotation of responsibilities. And it allows you to appoint someone to supervise the work group when you're absent.

Now that you've seen all the advantages of delegating, take a look at the flip side. When you fail to delegate, you steal from yourself, your family, your subordinates and your organization. Steal? Isn't that a strong word? Yes, it is, but failure to delegate is a serious offense.

Consequences of the Failure to Delegate

Examine how your failure to delegate becomes a thief of time, energy and motivation, which has an impact on many individuals. Trying to do it all yourself means you are:

- **Stealing from your subordinates.** Failure or refusal to delegate robs subordinates of initiative and job satisfaction. Chaos reigns. When methods become more important than results, the operation stagnates. No one has the power to decide or communicate. Everyone waits on the word from "upstairs." Rote work becomes easier the more it is repeated. Workers memorize their jobs like actors learn lines for a play. Boredom sets in.

  A large carpet store reached a point where a full-time assistant manager was required. The owner interviewed and hired a capable young business graduate from a local university. The assistant studied hard, kept busy and was a great help. After 18 months, the assistant gave notice and went to work for a competitive chain of retail stores. Why? The assistant had been busy but not responsible. The owner had failed truly to delegate. Delegation involves responsibility and authority, not just "busy work." Delegate, don't dump. Delegation must challenge the worker to grow and expand her horizons.

- **Stealing from the company.** When the $50-an-hour manager does a $20-an-hour job, the company is shortchanged $30 right away. Actually, the company is losing more than $30. Companies lose the chance for productivity and growth. If, instead, you spend a half-hour delegating and your subordinate spends four hours working on the task, you have effectively created up to eight times the result you would have had if you had not delegated.

  An associate came to the office of young Missouri Senator Harry Truman seeking a specific report. Truman's secretary was at lunch. Rather than tell the person that his secretary would find the document when she returned, Truman spent 30 minutes of his time looking for it. Only a few months later, he became president and had to shift into high gear. No longer could he waste time performing tasks someone else could and should easily do.

- **Stealing from yourself.** Ineffective delegation zaps the professional and personal lives of everyone. By delegating details, managers become specialists in the art of managing. They are not trapped by excelling at one task. They can walk into any division of a company prepared to make it function. They know people and how to develop them. They use people power to do the unique tasks of the department while they manage.

  Timothy Firnstahl, president of Restaurant Services, Inc. in Seattle, Washington, is a successful delegator. Within 36 months this young man moved up from serving cocktails to being a restaurant manager. He became a key member of the management team in a $15 million business.

- **Stealing from your family.** Ineffective delegation skills will also cramp your personal life. Do you stay late, take work home or feel that you are the only one who can handle the job? We all know people who "live" their jobs. They work late, rush lunches, lug work home and never take a vacation. These people fear a loss of control when they delegate. The effective manager doesn't need to know how a word processor works. She must understand what it does and how to delegate tasks to those who do understand how it works.

  John, carrying two briefcases, always arrived late for dinner. One night his 5-year-old daughter asked Mommy why Daddy had to carry two suitcases everywhere. Mommy proudly explained that Daddy was an executive with lots and lots of work to do. More work than he had time to do at the office. The child spoke to the heart of the matter: "Why don't they just put him in a slower group?" John had failed to switch from being a doer to a delegator.

Why Delegate?

- Delegation frees up your time and energy to perform at a higher level and allows greater clarity of vision by removing the "clutter."

- Delegation distributes responsibility to others and fosters team building. It creates a win-win situation for all involved.

- Delegation, properly handled, builds trust and others' skills and self-esteem.

- Delegation lends a new dimension as to how things can be done. New perspectives breathe new life into old problems.

- Delegation increases productivity, effectiveness and efficiency.

- Delegation presents a more professional, streamlined appearance to your superiors and the outside world.

Are You Doing the Right Job?

How well do you delegate? Are you doing the right job? Could improved delegation make your job more interesting and easier? Many quizzes have been devised to give managers a reading on how they rate as a delegator. The following checklist is representative of most. If your answer is "yes" to none or only one of these questions, you are doing fine as a delegator. If you answer "yes" to four or more of the questions, you could use improvement in your delegation skills.

_____ 1. Are you a perfectionist? Are you proud of it?

_____ 2. Do you take work home regularly?

_____ 3. Do you work longer hours than your subordinates?

_____ 4. Do you spend too much time doing tasks for others?

_____ 5. Do you often wish that you could spend more time with your family?

_____ 6. When you return to the office, is your "In" basket too full?

_____ 7. Do you still keep a hand in the job you held before your last promotion?

_____ 8. Are you often interrupted with queries or requests?

_____ 9. Can you immediately name your top three work goals?

_____ 10. Do you spend time on routine details that others could handle?

Reflections

_____ 11. Do you like to keep a finger in every pie?

_____ 12. Do you rush to meet deadlines?

_____ 13. Are you unable to keep on top of priorities?

_____ 14. Do you frequently feel overworked?

_____ 15. Is it hard for you to accept ideas offered by others?

_____ 16. Do you attract followers rather than leaders?

_____ 17. Do you give overly detailed instructions to subordinates?

_____ 18. Do you believe higher-level managers should work more?

_____ 19. Do you hold daily staff meetings?

_____ 20. Do you worry that your employees will show you up?

Reflections

3 BARRIERS TO DELEGATION

"It is often safer to be in chains than to be free."

— Franz Kafka

Delegation involves chance. Chance is risky. It is a question of control. When a job is delegated, there are feelings attached to the transfer of responsibility: loss of power, loss of authority, loss of achievement, etc. Even though some of these feelings are uncomfortable at times, the risk is worth it when you consider the benefits of delegation. Examining the barriers to delegation discussed throughout this chapter will help you develop your "delegation consciousness."

Barriers in the Manager

1. **I can do it better.** This fallacy of omnipotence is often found among managers. Even if the manager can do a better job, the choice is not between the quality of his work and the quality of the subordinate's; it is, rather, a choice between the benefits of his better performance on a single task and the benefits derived when he devotes that time to planning, delegating, supervising, training and developing a team. Eventually, such a team will both outperform and outlast the manager.

2. **Lack of patience/time.** "It takes longer to explain than to do it myself." That may be true, but it is also true of everything we teach our children as they grow up! Investing the time upfront to explain and train saves monumental amounts of time — and frustration — down the road. It also creates stronger, longer-lasting relationships as the skill levels of our subordinates (and children) broaden and deepen as a result.

3. **Lack of confidence in my subordinates.** This is a never-ending cycle. When delegation is withheld because of a lack of confidence, subordinates are denied the opportunity to develop the very abilities they need to warrant that confidence. This makes the manager's doubts a self-fulfilling prophecy.

4. **Insecurity.** Newly promoted managers are often uncomfortable in their new jobs … and can't resist going back to tell their replacement how to proceed. They may fear losing their control, authority and/or power.

5. **Anxiety.** Many managers refuse to delegate anything to anyone as they endeavor to "prove themselves."

6. **Fear of rejection.** Do not be afraid of being disliked by subordinates. Delegation is not tyranny. Don't be afraid to ask others to increase their job responsibilities. Also, don't be afraid that you will appear to be dispensable to the company. Delegation is a management tool designed to help you get greater results with less effort. Hectic pace is not a sign of achievement, but of inefficiency.

7. **Feelings of inadequacy.** "What if I delegate this project and Joe does it so well he shows me up? Do I really want my management to see that he can do these things better than I can?"

8. **Inflexibility.** "This is something I've always done and always will."

9. **Occupational hobbies.** Some managers get so involved in "pet" projects that they refuse to let them go, regardless of their

negative impact on the manager's overall time and resource-management effectiveness.

Manager's Excuses for Not Delegating

"It takes too long to explain."

"No one on my staff is capable of doing it."

"If you want it done right, you have to do it yourself."

"My people are already overworked. I can't dump anything more on them."

Barriers in the Subordinate

1. **Lack of experience/competence.** Your subordinates may not be prepared to do the tasks that you want to assign to them. They may lack skills and experience. Perhaps the best thing to do is to make changes. You might replace those who are unskilled. Another way to solve the problem is to use delegation as a form of training. Begin with the assignment of simple, routine tasks. Step by step, develop each subordinate's level of skill and competence. It takes great patience, but it can be done.

2. **Avoidance of responsibility.** Go slowly. Clarify your ideas of delegation as you extend the scope of your delegating. As subordinates see the advantages they gain in the process, their resistance will vanish. Fashioning a series of small successes is the best way to handle these cases. Each delegation should help the employee build up confidence for the next one.

3. **Resentment.** When employees feel "dumped" upon — being told to do the "boss's job" without a clear understanding of the personal benefits to them — resentment develops and increased resistance to delegation occurs.

4. **Fear.** Many employees fear criticism or embarrassment if they
   don't do things exactly as the boss expects. The more autocratic
   and dictatorial the boss, the greater (and more valid) the fear. The
   better the relationship between manager and subordinate, the more
   manageable this concern becomes.

5. **Lack of recognition.** When an employee feels good work has gone
   unacknowledged, unrecognized and unrewarded in the past, what
   incentive does he have to take on additional responsibilities?
   Overcome this barrier by developing a systematic way of publicly
   recognizing each individual's contributions.

The Real Reasons Managers Don't Delegate

"I'm comfortable doing the job I've been doing for a long time. If I
give that up, then I have to concentrate on the responsibilities of my
new job, which I am not comfortable with."

"If someone else can do my job, maybe I won't be needed anymore."

"I'm the boss; I'm supposed to have control over everything."

"What if the other person messes up? I'm still accountable."

Barriers in the Situation

1. **Lack of organization.** When your boss assigns a task to one of
   your subordinates without telling you, chaos is the immediate result.
   You can no longer effectively delegate to that subordinate. What
   you must do is sit down with your boss and come to some mutual
   understanding of your duties and those of each of your subordinates.
   Discuss the company's or department's organizational chart with
   him. Explain the confusion that results when he shoots from the hip
   in handing out assignments.

2. **Staffing problems.** Having an insufficient staff of overworked subordinates can be a big stumbling block when seeking to delegate. But it's not an impossible situation. Do whatever you must do in an effort to hire additional people. This can mean taking on an additional staff member or two or hiring specialists from the outside. If you're not able to add people, check the subordinates you do have. Are they using their time efficiently? Are they delegating to their subordinates? In most cases, you shouldn't worry about the situation; delegate anyway. You're almost sure to find that your subordinates are flexible enough to handle the additional work.

Ten Secrets of Successful, Effective Delegation

1. Know your employees — their strengths, weaknesses and skill levels.

2. Delegate to someone known to be responsible and accountable.

3. Customize a reward/incentive package, if appropriate.

4. Establish goals, objectives, expectations and time frames.

5. Identify the indicators of failure. Identify consequences for poor performance.

6. Encourage creativity and independence.

7. Focus on results.

8. Develop an ironclad reporting system, and follow up regularly.

9. Provide adequate resources and support.

10. Review and celebrate successes.

Are you delegating enough? Affirmative answers to the majority of the following questions indicate significant barriers are interfering with your delegation.

Yes	No	
_____	_____	Do you often work overtime?
_____	_____	Do you take work home evenings and weekends?
_____	_____	Is your unfinished work increasing?
_____	_____	Are daily operations so time-consuming that you have little time left for planning and other important matters?
_____	_____	Do you have to control all the details to have a job done right?
_____	_____	Do you frequently have to postpone long-range projects?
_____	_____	Are you harassed by constant unexpected emergencies?
_____	_____	Do you lack confidence in your subordinates' abilities to shoulder more responsibility?
_____	_____	Do you find yourself irritable and complaining when the work of your group doesn't live up to expectations?
_____	_____	Do conflict, friction and loss of morale characterize the atmosphere of your work group?
_____	_____	Do your subordinates defer all decisions to you?
_____	_____	Do you instruct your subordinates to perform certain activities, rather than to accomplish certain goals?
_____	_____	Have subordinates stopped presenting their ideas to you?
_____	_____	Do operations slow down much when you are away?
_____	_____	Do you feel that you're abdicating your role as a manager if you ask for assistance from your subordinates?
_____	_____	Do you believe that your status and the salary you earn automatically mean that you have to be overworked?

Reflections

4 WHAT TO DELEGATE

"What is worth doing is worth the trouble of asking somebody to do it."

— Ambrose Bierce

"A good staff will find the work to do." Ridiculous. Why should the staff "find" work to do? That's your job now — managing and directing work. Even though people sometimes slide through their workday, there's no reason you should choose inefficient and often directionless management. In this chapter, we will identify categories and types of tasks that are good candidates for delegation.

If you're blessed with a legion of self-starters, you're lucky. However, in general, unless you think of yourself as the main source of new work for your staff, few new things will be done. Encouraging the "busy look" merely ensures old tasks will be done with increasingly less efficiency. Every manager should strive to make herself dispensable to the operation of her company. Successful delegation develops the maximum potential of your team to such a point. As a manager, the important thing is not what happens when you are there but what happens when you are not there. The very drive and determination that earmark successful workers, however, are often the same qualities that hinder effective delegation. Outperforming a subordinate on a specific task is not the issue. The choice is a comparative advantage between managerial success on one specific task and the successful coaching, planning and directing (managing) of an entire team.

Since your own work forms the main source of responsibilities to be delegated, making a detailed list of the jobs you do is crucial. The key word is "detailed." Unfortunately, most work does not fall neatly into specific categories of delegation. How then do you decide what to delegate and what not to delegate? The following guidelines might help you decide:

1. **Delegate the routine and the necessary tasks.** These are the jobs that you have done over and over. These are often the necessary tasks of the job that are routinely dictated by your company. You know them. You know the problems, the peculiarities and the specifics of how to do these jobs. These are the easiest jobs to delegate. Because you know these tasks so well, you can easily explain and delegate them away.

   Are you required to attend regularly scheduled "informational meetings" that could easily be handled by your subordinates? For the past several years, a local bank vice president was required to attend a monthly council luncheon of all financial institutions in the community. These luncheons were primarily social and rarely yielded anything that could not have been handled by the vice president's assistant. The vice president realized that this was a "doing" job, not a "planning" job. She called in the assistant vice president of the bank and explained the function of this meeting. The young assistant was enthusiastic and eager for a chance to meet her colleagues in a professional setting. This was the perfect opportunity for successful delegation.

2. **Delegate the specialties.** Would you perform surgery on your family? Probably not, unless you happen to be a surgeon. Would you represent yourself in court without a lawyer? Probably not, unless you happen to be a lawyer. You would look for the most skilled person in the field. The same is true in the office. Take advantage of any specialties that exist in your office. If you are responsible for choosing a new word-processing system, you could do the research yourself — or you could delegate the initial research to the computer programmer in your office. If you have a math

whiz in the office, that person could assume the responsibility of double-checking the math in all the reports.

Beware of the "Superman Syndrome." Realize that there are occasions that require delegation of tasks you normally perform to skilled professionals such as lawyers, accountants, tax preparers and temporary "overload" employees. At such times, make sure to check references for the best possible person. Don't just reach for the phone directory. Match your need to the skills of the people available to you. Practice selective delegation here.

3. **Delegate "occupational hobbies."** These are the duties you should have delegated a long time ago but haven't because they're too much fun. It's okay to keep a couple, but at least recognize them for what they are: easy and enjoyable ... and much better done by somebody else. It may seem paradoxical to delegate the very aspects of your job that you enjoy most. Yet these are often the tasks that you hang on to even though they don't represent the best use of your time and energy. They are often related to your area of expertise or earlier positions that you have had with the company. Andrew Sigler, chairman of Champion International, refers to this as "Turf Mentality." Holding on to specific duties becomes a manager's means of protecting her turf.

A sales manager has been attending the same trade show in Chicago each year for several years. She looks upon the assignment as a chance to get away and see old friends. Actually it's no longer necessary for the sales manager to be there. One of her sales representatives could achieve the same results. Do you see yourself in this or comparable situations? Are you simply indulging yourself? Wouldn't your career be better served by spending the time at your desk? Take a look at your priorities.

4. **Delegate problems or issues that require exploration, study and recommendations for decisions.** Your job is to ensure that the ultimate decision is made correctly and the plan executed effectively — not to explore and study alternative courses of action.

5. **Delegate tasks that tap human talent in a positive direction — toward organizational goals and needs and toward the person's development and growth.** With selective delegation, you can match specific individuals with growth opportunities. Delegating a task for which an individual has a partial skill or qualification is a great place to start. People are wonderful resources to be utilized and enjoy being recognized for their personal strengths and abilities.

6. **Delegate a task specifically requested by a subordinate.** If someone expresses an interest in a task you have half completed, hand it over. She will likely be highly motivated, committed and enthusiastic about completing it!

Effective Delegation

- Determine the type of work to be assigned.

- Identify the result required.

- Establish limits.

- Provide examples of success.

- Prepare a delegation worksheet.

- Gain commitment.

- Monitor progress.

- Reward results.

Would you do it yourself … or delegate?	**Do It Myself**	**Delegate**
1. Represent your group in routine meetings.		
2. Open and sort today's mail.		
3. Decide on a new intercom system.		
4. Schedule your out-of-town appointments.		
5. Write an interoffice memo.		
6. Arrange for refreshments at a meeting.		
7. Follow up on your phone messages.		
8. Arrange for temporary help.		
9. Brainstorm new ideas.		
10. Handle a personnel problem.		
11. Handle routine office personnel chores.		
12. Submit objectives for your department.		
13. Read relevant trade journals and books.		
14. Work on the group's budget.		
15. Be interviewed for a work-related magazine article.		
16. Give orientation to a new employee.		
17. Interview/hire additional help.		
18. Schedule vacations.		
19. Plan an advertising campaign.		

Reflections

5 WHAT NOT TO DELEGATE

"The buck stops with the guy who signs the checks."

— Rupert Murdoch

While the majority of managers err on the side of not delegating enough of their workload, there is the occasional manager who delegates entirely too much. For many reasons, there are certain tasks that simply cannot be delegated to your subordinates. This chapter provides a cautionary look at items that should *not* be delegated as a general rule.

Executives, from CEOs on down, do have obligations and responsibilities that are not to be delegated. These are among the very reasons that you have your job rather than a subordinate position.

1. **Don't delegate rituals.** There are certain functions that require a person of specific position to be present. Retiring employees don't expect to have their retirement gifts presented by the president's secretary. They expect and deserve to have someone as important as the president in attendance.

   When a local church applied for a building permit, the congregation's lawyer could have represented them at the zoning hearing. However, in a town where most people knew each other, the minister realized that his presence at the meeting — in addition to the lawyer's — would be important. His presence signified the importance of this building to the church and the community.

2. **Don't delegate personnel/confidential matters.** Personnel decisions (evaluation, promotion or dismissal) are generally "touchy" and often difficult decisions to make. While you may need the confidential input of your subordinates on personnel issues, the job and responsibility are yours.

   While an analysis of your department's job classifications and pay scales may seem time-consuming and a prime job for delegation, this is a job for management. Imagine the problems in maintaining the confidentiality of all salaries within a department. This is not a job to delegate to your subordinates.

3. **Don't delegate policy-making.** Responsibilities and tasks within a certain policy area can be delegated, but never delegate the actual formulation of a policy. Policy sets the limits of decision-making.

   Responsibility for policy-making within specified, limited guidelines, however, may be delegated. General credit policies of businesses are developed by credit managers, yet the ability to grant credit to specific customers up to certain dollar limits is often granted to salesmen.

4. **Don't delegate crises.** Crises will inevitably happen. A crisis does not offer the time for initiating delegation. When one does occur, it is the responsibility of the manager to shoulder the problem and find the solution. Studies have shown that in times of crisis and heavy workloads, successful delegators maintain their leadership roles. This is because they have laid the groundwork for delegation prior to the onset of the crisis. Their subordinates are self-motivated and enthusiastic team players. They know what to expect. They are part of a trained team. A crisis in business demands skill and experience.

   The manager of a plumbing contracting company discovered that his major client urgently needed cost projections from the company before construction bids for a multimillion-dollar project could be submitted. The computers for the local contractor's supply house were down that day. The manager faced a crisis. He was the one who had to make decisions, deal with the general building contractor, determine the availability of parts from other suppliers, etc.

When the heat is on, make sure that you are there to take the lead.

5. **Don't delegate tasks that should be eliminated.** All too often, reports continue to be written or the effort of another group is duplicated simply because "we've always done it that way." Tasks and activities in your organization that do not contribute to the firm's goals and objectives — that do not provide an appropriate cost/benefit ratio — must be identified and eliminated. Delegating these useless tasks to your subordinates will cause morale and commitment problems.

6. **Don't delegate tasks you would not be willing to do yourself.** You will lose credibility and respect if you delegate tasks you have not done — or would not do — yourself. In other words, don't delegate all the unpleasant work and keep the fun things for yourself.

7. **Don't delegate planning.** Don't ask your subordinates to develop plans for which they do not have the training, insight or responsibility. Involve your subordinates, definitely. But the long-term direction and performance of your group is your personal responsibility. Solicit and utilize input from members of your team, then make the strategic decisions yourself.

8. **Don't delegate morale problems.** You need the support and cooperation of your entire team, but the responsibility for maintaining good morale is the manager's job. Establishing behavioral guidelines, watching carefully for early warning signs of discontent and acting quickly to nip problems in the bud are not tasks you can delegate. As issues arise — either with an individual team member or with the group as a whole — address them directly … and personally.

9. **Don't delegate reconciliation of differences between line and staff members.** In many organizations, these differences are systemic. The resentments and misunderstandings regarding each group's value to the organization can be a problem of long standing. Be sure you are personally involved in developing a stronger rapport between these groups. Keep your negotiation and mediation skills sharp.

10. **Don't delegate a direct assignment that your boss has specifically given you to complete.** The boss gave it to you because he wanted you to do it. When accepting delegations from above, be sure that you are clear on which items must be done by someone (anyone) in your group and which ones require your personal attention.

11. **Don't delegate matters for which there is not enough qualified talent available.** Be sure your delegatees have the necessary skills to be successful or have access to the training to develop these skills. If delegating a "developmental" task, review the timetable carefully to ensure you have allowed sufficient time for training and project completion. Set your people up to succeed, not to fail.

12. **Don't delegate "pet" projects, ideas or activities when they do not interfere with your larger duties.** If the item is truly one of your "pets," you won't be able to resist meddling in your subordinate's work. If you can't let it go, don't delegate it.

1. What tasks/activities have you delegated in the past that, in retrospect, you realize were among the "Don't Delegate" group?

2. Review all the tasks completed by your group to assess if any can be eliminated.

   - Who are the recipients of the report, task, service, etc.?

   - How does it help them?

   - Does this effort duplicate something another group is doing?

   - What would be the consequences if you eliminated it?

   - How does it contribute to the organization's goals and objectives?

   - Is the benefit worth the cost?

3. What steps do you need to take to eliminate the items identified in #2 above?

4. What other changes do you expect to see one year from now as a result of what you learned in this chapter?

Reflections

6 PLANNING WHAT TO DELEGATE

"There is nothing so useless as doing efficiently that which should not be done at all."

— Peter Drucker

Knowing that you need to delegate is easy. Unless you plan to work yourself to death for the glory of the company, you will be happy to give away some of your jobs. What jobs? How do you decide? The dual-step framework in which to make these decisions is the focus of this chapter:

Step 1. Analyze and assess your job.

Step 2. Analyze and assess your subordinates.

Step 1: Analyze and Assess Your Job

Since your job responsibilities are the wellspring of work for your subordinates, you must analyze your job. Are there tasks that initially helped you learn to do the job? Are there jobs that others need to know in order to keep the unit functioning when you're gone? These are definitely jobs that you can successfully delegate to your subordinates. By delegating, you keep yourself growing. You keep your people growing too. Just because you're bored with a task doesn't mean it couldn't be a wonderful challenge for someone else.

There are some simple steps that will help you to decide which jobs to delegate:

1. List all the jobs (results and their components) that you are responsible for.

2. For two weeks, keep a separate running list of all you do during the day. (Include everything, even answering the phone during lunch breaks.)

3. List a time estimate for each task.

4. Review all your personnel — their skills and attributes.

5. Place the name of a staff member by each task, matching skills and attributes with the needs of each task.

6. Make a list of all the details and instructions an employee will need to accomplish each task.

7. Decide on checks and balances (evaluation controls) for each task.

8. Determine alternative time frames for each task (in case the job needs to be redone or is not finished on time).

Step 2: Analyze and Assess Your Subordinates

Having analyzed and assessed your work, the next step is to analyze and assess the capabilities of your subordinates. It is essential to present subordinates with challenges that fit their next level of growth. An under-challenged person will quickly become bored. Overchallenge and you'll have a very frustrated, unhappy employee. Mastering this is more an art than a science, but there is one easy way of improving your accuracy. Look at your people. Who's been hinting for more challenge? Open your mind to people who may not seem qualified — often an ounce of enthusiasm is worth a pound of experience. Creative delegation sends a good signal that people in your organization can shape their own futures.

The following checklist can help you decide what kind of project to delegate to a particular subordinate.

Work Style Profile

1. Does she work quickly or slowly?

2. Does she seek out new assignments?

3. Does she require minimal or maximum direction?

4. Does she make a lot of mistakes or only a few mistakes?

5. Does she write well or poorly?

6. Is she organized or disorganized?

7. Does she like working alone or with others?

8. Does she prefer structured work or the opportunity for creativity?

9. Does she give strong verbal presentations?

10. Does she handle large assignments well?

This analysis is not something to use to make decisions about raises, promotions and transfers. Unless you supervise an assembly line, you have a sufficient variety of tasks to interest anyone. Some tasks require speed, others don't. Some require good oral presentation skills, others can be performed without a word being spoken. Some projects require careful thought and analysis, others are simple and straightforward.

Even employees who resist new assignments can and should be delegated to. It's your responsibility to define tasks that fall within the scope of the person's existing abilities and will reasonably stretch those skills in the training process. So, we come right back to the foundation of delegation: your ability to define jobs and creatively match those jobs to your staff.

Delegation — Things to Remember

- Remember that a person may need a different reporting system depending on the project.

- Remember to give all the information needed to complete the project successfully.

- Remember to define the level of authority you are giving the individual.

- Remember to be available for the individual's questions.

- Remember to reward the employee for a job well done.

- Remember that saying thanks is a neglected form of compensation.

1. Complete both of the planning steps as outlined in this chapter.

    Step 1: Analyze and assess your job. Use the eight questions on page 38 as a guide.

    Step 2: Analyze and assess your subordinates. Use the 10 questions on page 39.

2. After completing #1 above, complete the Delegation Opportunities Worksheet below.

Delegation Opportunities Worksheet

What I Do	Delegate (Yes/No)	To Whom	Preparation Time
1.			
2.			
3.			
4.			
5.			
6.			
7.			
8.			
9.			
10.			

Reflections

7 EFFECTIVE GOAL-SETTING IN THE DELEGATION PROCESS

"You've got to be very careful if you don't know where you are going, because you might not get there."

— Yogi Berra

The common injunction to "do your best" is virtually useless in motivating people. Actually, if we think about it, this finding is not surprising at all. Ambiguity is the antithesis of productivity. What does "do your best" mean? To the worker faced daily with countless variables and demands, it means dozens of things — and because the worker hears it all the time, it comes to mean nothing at all. Establishing clear expectations and setting specific goals are the central issues of this chapter.

The Role of Expectations and Goals

Expectations and goals must be specific, clearly stated and clearly measurable. Goals with these characteristics provide a source of feedback, accountability and evaluation. Well-stated, measurable objectives are invaluable in motivating people and improving their performance. If an employee does not have a clear idea of the task at hand and does not receive feedback on his performance of it, he cannot realistically be accountable for the task. Nevertheless, the chaotic workplace, where no one really knows what to do and seldom gets feedback on what is or is not being done effectively, is more prevalent in American business.

Goals must be measurable in order to be effective. It's also worthwhile to remember that people understand and respond to quantity more than quality. If you must choose between them while you're defining your goals, go for "more" rather than "better."

Let's be even more concrete. Sound objectives have three identifiable elements:

1. An action verb (to increase, to contact, to sell, to enroll, etc.)

2. A measurable result (five, 50 percent, 3,000, etc.)

3. The date by which the objective will be accomplished (3 p.m. on June 16).

In the beginning, set your goals for a "marginal" employee with one view in mind: to build successes. Even though the employee will eventually perform at a higher level, don't expect immediate results. Aim for just a little bit more work than the employee has been doing; aim for what he might succeed in reaching. Success builds on success. If you want a successful performer to do more, don't be afraid to aim high.

A time element is crucial to commitments. Ask and agree upon a time for completion. Do not say, "I want you to get your work done soon." Instead say, "The goal is to increase production 10 percent by June 16." And whatever you do, avoid saying, "Why don't we get together sometime soon and discuss this again." Rather say, "Let's get together on March 3 at 3 p.m. for a review of our progress." Establish with your employee the understanding that commitments can be renegotiated, but don't be open-ended about it. Getting a firm commitment takes time on your part, but it is an essential element in good supervision.

Without commitment to success, the best-laid plans are often doomed to failure. Therefore it is crucial to get your employees committed to the goals. Too often we take commitment for granted and overlook this simple step. You want more than nodded approval or tacit acceptance. Go for an outright statement that the person agrees on the goals and the deadlines. Be prepared to include employee suggestions or modifications in your goals and deadlines. Be flexible. If you have spent considerable time working out a plan in some detail, it makes sense to spend a few more minutes to secure a commitment from your employee that he will put the plan into action.

Even when a plan seems quite workable, you might want to get a written commitment. Many management experts suggest that each goal and its measurable performance standard be written out on paper. Each goal and its evaluation measure should take no more than 250 words or one side of one piece of paper. Place the accountability where it belongs. Train yourself and your subordinates to review these written goals on a regular basis.

Keys to Avoiding Common Errors in Goal Setting

- Carefully clarify common objectives for the entire group.
- Set goals high enough to challenge the employees.
- Use prior results to find new and unusual goal combinations.
- Blend the team's common objectives with those of the whole organization.
- Cluster responsibilities in the most appropriate positions.
- Clearly define who is responsible for what.
- Avoid duplication of effort and responsibility.
- Stress results and responsibility — not methods or process.
- Limit the number and scope of goals to increase likelihood of success.
- Create a plan for successful completion of each goal.
- Use policies as action guides. Do not use ad hoc judgments.
- Bring in new ideas from outside the organization.
- Identify and implement the support that management needs to provide.
- Establish milestones by which progress is measured.
- Reinforce successful behavior when goals are achieved.

Matching the Goal and the Delegatee

To properly set delegation goals, you must know your subordinates well. What are their individual strengths, weaknesses, personal goals and fears? How do the tasks at hand fit? A task or goal that fits one individual may be totally wrong for another. Also, consider the delegatee when choosing a delegation goal.

To delegate effectively, you must match people with appropriate goals. If you force an unsuitable goal on an individual, you discourage that individual and lower morale. Delegation is a process that requires thought, planning and sensitivity to the needs of both the individuals and the organization.

Talk with your people when you begin to plan a delegation. Get their input. Frequently, ideas will emerge that will help you set better goals and make better delegation selections. Together you can evaluate the level of challenge of the task at hand and the degree of control the delegatee will need for completion.

Five Ways to Reach a Goal Faster

1. Break the goal down into important pieces. Relish the momentum as you accomplish each one.

2. Tie the goal to one of your core values, so it becomes an expression of yourself rather than just a "thing" you are working on.

3. Reward yourself along the way. Refresh and revive your energy and dedication.

4. Act as if you have already achieved the goal, and do what it takes to "polish it off."

5. Install a consequence that really, really hurts.

Using the three elements of sound objectives — action verbs, measurable result and timeline — write five clear goals for your people to pursue.

Goal: _____

_____

Evaluation method: _____

_____

Goal: _____

_____

Evaluation method: _____

_____

Goal: _____

_____

Evaluation method: _____

_____

Goal: _____

_____

Evaluation method: _____

_____

Goal: _____

_____

Evaluation method: _____

_____

Reflections

Reflections

8 CHOOSING A DELEGATEE

"No duty the Executive had to perform was so trying as to put the right man in the right place."

— Thomas Jefferson

You've determined what you are going to delegate. You've taken the time to plan how you are going to present the task, including your requirements, parameters, authority level, feedback needs and specific expectations. It's all in writing to minimize miscommunication. This chapter addresses the next step — selecting the appropriate delegatee.

Consider this scenario: "Jenny, you've been a medical supply salesperson for our company for the past five years. You've done such a good job as a salesperson — perfect attendance, punctuality, excellent customer relations skills and knowledge of pharmaceuticals — that we want you to come in next week and be a doctor. So here are the keys to Operating Room 9. Feel free to move in. Now don't worry about a thing. We have confidence in you, and we'll be there all the way to back you up. Just put on this new stethoscope and pick out some supplies for this medical bag. Get a good feel for the job and get to know the nursing staff.

"If this is the job for you, we'll enroll you in a correspondence program offered through the local college. It's called 'The Theoretical Practice of Medicine.' You'll study medical history, human anatomy and physician penmanship. You'll learn patient billing and selection of malpractice insurance. After three years, we'll teach you how to operate on people."

Thankfully, physicians and surgeons aren't trained that way. Yet similar scenarios are played out daily in the business world. Authority is granted to employees precisely because they are so good at their nonauthority jobs. They are terrific, so promote them. But too often, the boss forgets to teach them how to do the job.

In many hospitals, for instance, nurses are promoted to department heads with next to no training. They are told one day, "You're the boss." The next day they have a cluttered office and must figure out what they're supposed to do. Think of the excellent salespeople who have been promoted to sales manager and were left to sink or swim.

Selection of delegatees has three general goals. In choosing the right delegatee, weigh these goals to determine which are the most important to the task at hand. It's a decision similar to that of a presidential candidate selecting a running mate. The person selected must be competent. However, the candidate must also consider such diverse factors as balancing the ticket and patching up party rivalries.

The three general goals to consider in delegatee selection are:

1. **Direct results.** For most cases of delegation, the direct result is the most important goal. (But keep in mind the two other important goals of delegation.)

    Mr. Addison of Acme Supply has called demanding to know where his 600 cases of widgets are. If the missing widgets are not accounted for within 24 hours, he's threatening to cancel the order. Both Sharon and Sam are capable of tracking the missing widgets. However, Sharon has more experience at tracking diverted orders, plus she has dealt with Mr. Addison and his secretary in the past. So even though Sam could do the job, you opt for Sharon this time. She is obviously more proficient and suited to this particular delegation opportunity.

2. **Development.** Development of employee skills always represents an important delegation goal. It also complicates the selection of the delegatee. You want the right person, not necessarily the most

competent person. Surprisingly, there are numerous opportunities to delegate tasks where the goal of developing the delegatee's skills is paramount and the direct result is of lesser consequence. People who are normally half-dead from boredom or frustration during office hours come alive when given a new challenge, and their abilities take a quantum leap. It's far better to have champions working for you than zombies.

Realizing that Mr. Addison of Acme Supply is a major customer, you know that it is important for your entire staff to handle his account with the proper concern and respect. From the first day that Sam joins your staff as an accounting clerk/typist, you begin to explain the importance of the Acme account. Even though Sharon can handle these routine transactions of billing, shipping and accounting for the Acme orders (she's done it for years), you begin to delegate the Acme transactions to Sam. Eventually, Mr. Addison will call with a rush order or a temper tantrum as he is prone to do. When the crisis comes, Sam will be ready to respond because you have developed his skills slowly but surely.

3. **Evaluation.** Sooner or later subordinates will have to be tested under fire. In some delegations, your main goal is to observe individual performance in a given situation. Be careful not to delegate with the expectation of failure. To do so would eventually reflect unfavorably on you. Delegation does provide indications of employees' strengths and weaknesses that would not otherwise be apparent to managers.

The manager of a local food brokerage firm needed to fill an account representative's position. She asked her secretary to assist another experienced account representative with the setup of a brand-new supermarket. While the job was accomplished in an acceptable manner, the secretary realized that this job was not for her. The working conditions, travel, hours and other things were not what she wanted in a job. Both parties were able to make some important long-term assessments based on this delegation.

Delegation is a useful tool in determining the future potential of employees in the work force. It is a mutually beneficial way of allowing the employee to explore all facets of the work done in your business.

Assessing the Personalities of Potential Delegatees

The personality and underlying attitude of each of your subordinates must also be considered when selecting the proper delegatee for a particular task. While there are as many personalities as there are individuals, here are some specific types to be on the lookout for:

- Workhorse

- One-Man Band

- Know-It-All

- No Way, Jack!

- Who Cares, Anyway?

Workhorse: This individual is dedicated and committed ... and probably a perfectionist. She works long hours and her world seems to revolve around her work. The old adage, "If you want something done right, give it to a busy person" applies here. The Workhorse is always busy, always overloaded. Before delegating to the Workhorse, be sure you:

- Discuss priorities.

- Identify specific tasks and detailed timelines.

- Specify expectations regarding quality and amount of time to be devoted.

One-Man Band: This individual is extremely capable and likely to take on additional responsibilities. Chances are she will volunteer for more than her fair share of the work. As with the Workhorse, it is tempting to toss the assignment into these willing and capable hands. But, before you do:

- Evaluate the number of tasks this person is already responsible for. The One-Man Band tends to get overcommitted … and burned out.

- Consider asking this person to mentor a less experienced member of your team in handling this assignment.

Know-It-All: While this person may, indeed, be extremely knowledgeable in some areas, she will claim to have expertise in areas in which she really has none. Having this person on your team can be a mixed blessing.

- Capitalize on her knowledge by delegating appropriate projects in which this expertise can be utilized most fully.

- Do your homework in order to accurately assess the true level of expertise vs. that professed by the Know-It-All. Ask questions. Challenge statements.

- Watch for personality conflicts between this person and others on your team. The Know-It-All is annoying to many people.

No Way, Jack!: Also known as Ms. Negativity, this ray of sunshine sees the worst possible aspect of everything. She'll no doubt have countless reasons why the project won't work or why she simply can't be the one to handle it.

- Set this person up to succeed. Be very clear about your expectations and performance standards.

- Set up a rigorous follow-up system to keep the project positive and on track. If you don't, your "Negative Nellie" can make the prediction of failure a self-fulfilling prophecy.

Who Cares, Anyway?: Perhaps the most challenging of all is the subordinate who just doesn't care anymore. They feel their contributions are not valued and/or that the work itself is meaningless.

- Listen carefully to this individual's comments and read between the lines. You may just pick up some clues about what will motivate her.

- Be a coach, not a crutch. Require performance. Challenge with humor.

- Publicly praise contributions (and effort).

Keep these ideas in mind when selecting a delegatee:

- Pick people who are reliable and know how to handle responsibility.

- Make sure the tasks are matched to the individuals in those areas where they have expertise and are efficient in performing them.

- Acknowledge to yourself and to the delegatee that she may not handle tasks the same way you would (and perhaps not as efficiently).

- Be sure to listen to the ideas of the people to whom you are delegating and allow them to stamp their own personalities on the project.

- Ease new delegatees into the process with simple tasks and build up from there.

- Provide full and complete information to each delegatee — notes, ideas, objectives, constraints, pitfalls and deadlines.

- Follow up as needed to ensure each party's comfort level and to ensure success.

Task Analysis and Delegatee Selection

Task/activity: _____

Direct results required: _____

_____

_____

Employees who *could* achieve direct results:

_____

_____

Person *most likely* to achieve direct results:

_____

_____

Employees for whom task/activity could be used for *development*:

_____

_____

Employees for whom task/activity could be used for *evaluation*:

_____

_____

Considering the direct results required and the development and
evaluation factors above, select the right person for the task/activity:

_____

Reflections

1. Identify a responsibility that you normally have but would like to delegate to someone else.

2. Identify the person to whom you will delegate responsibility. Why did you choose this person? What are this person's skills, experience and personality issues that make this a good delegation fit?

3. Outline the specific tasks to be done.

4. Define expectations and performance standards.

5. Schedule a delegation conference with this individual.

6. When you have successfully completed the delegation detailed above, select another responsibility, and repeat the process.

Reflections

Reflections

9 DEVELOPING PEOPLE POWER THROUGH DELEGATION

"You see, really and truly, apart from the things anyone can pick up (the dressing and the proper way of speaking and so on), the difference between a lady and a flower girl is not how she behaves, but how she's treated. I shall always be a flower girl to Professor Higgins, because he always treats me as a flower girl and always will, but I know I can be a lady to you, because you always treat me as a lady and always will."

— Eliza Doolittle in George Bernard Shaw's *Pygmalion*

Like Professor Higgins, most managers unintentionally treat their subordinates in a way that leads to less-than-desirable performance. Many leaders have difficulty delegating responsibility. There seems to be the programmed feeling that the only way to get the job done right is to do it yourself. While doing it yourself may appear to work, it tends to be a breeding ground for apathy, noninvolvement, low motivation and loss of commitment and enthusiasm. Sharing the work can be a great motivator, thereby strengthening the organization. This chapter is devoted to the personnel development aspects of delegation.

The way managers treat their subordinates is subtly influenced by what they expect of them. If a manager's expectations are high, productivity is likely to be high. If his expectations are low, productivity is likely to be low. It is as though there is a law that causes a subordinate's performance to rise or fall to meet his manager's expectations.

J. Sterling Livingston of the Harvard Business School describes the "Pygmalion in Management Effect" this way:

1. **What a manager expects of a subordinate and how he treats the subordinate will combine to profoundly influence the subordinate's performance and his career progress.** What is critical in the communication of expectations is not what the boss says, but what he does. Indifference and noncommittal treatment communicate low expectations and lead to inferior performance. Most managers are more effective in communicating low expectations to their subordinates than in communicating high expectations, even though most managers believe exactly the opposite.

2. **Superior managers create high performance expectations that subordinates can fulfill.** Subordinates will not strive for high productivity unless they consider the boss's high expectations realistic and achievable. If they are pushed to strive for unattainable goals, they eventually give up trying. Frustrated, they settle for results that are lower than they are capable of achieving. The experience of a large printing company demonstrates this. The company discovered that production actually declined if production quotas were set too high, because the workers simply stopped trying to meet them. "Dangling the carrot just beyond the donkey's reach" is not a good motivational device.

3. **Less effective managers fail to develop high expectations for their subordinates.** Successful managers have greater confidence than ineffective managers in their ability to develop the talents of subordinates. The successful manager's record of achievement and self-confidence grant credibility to his goals. Thus, subordinates accept his expectations as realistic and try hard to achieve them.

What Motivates Employees

Integral to the success of delegation is the development of employees' self-esteem. The use of self-esteem as a motivator is a recent phenomenon. In the 1930s the issue was irrelevant. Back then, the issues were money, security and survival — the very things that were in short supply. Recent distinct improvements in the satisfaction of these survival needs have brought with them a whole new set of drives. Workers have begun to complain about a lack of dignity and respect. With increasing turnover rates, absenteeism and other forms of alienation and dissatisfaction, managers can no longer maintain that workers only care about getting a paycheck.

- Delegation helps people below you in the organization grow and thereby pushes you even higher in management. It provides you with more time to take on higher-priority projects.

- Find out what the talents and interests of your people are and you will be able to delegate more intelligently and effectively.

- Never underestimate a person's potential. Delegate slightly more than what you think the person is capable of handling. Expect them to succeed, and you will be pleasantly surprised more often than not.

- Clearly define what outcome is needed, then let individuals use their own creative thinking to determine how to get that outcome.

- Clearly define the limits of authority that go with the delegated job. Can the person hire other people to work with them? What are the spending constraints?

- Do not avoid delegating something because you cannot give someone the entire project. Let the person start with a bite-sized piece. After learning and doing that portion, they can accept larger pieces and areas of responsibility.

- Clear standards of performance will help the person know when he is doing exactly what is expected.

- Delegation is taking a risk that the other person might make a mistake. People learn from mistakes … and will be able to do the project correctly the next time. Where would you be if no one had ever taken a chance on you?

The fact is that management experts and psychologists have shown that a salary increase is not necessarily the ultimate motivator. Unless you cannot live on your present salary, more money is often a weak incentive. In addition to providing money to live on, most people work every day to satisfy their need for structure and predictability in their lives. Look at the endless number of rich men who continue to work every day. Precisely because their basic needs are being met, workers today do not automatically accept authoritarian, dehumanizing styles of management.

Workers' priorities have changed. Statistics show that such benefits as interesting work, sufficient help, adequate equipment and information to get the job done and enough authority/independence to do the job are as important to workers as good pay. None of these newly demanded features is a tangible economic benefit. Rather, each of them is either a subtle or direct result of the need for self-esteem.

In the 1950s, Dr. Abraham Maslow defined and listed a hierarchy of human needs. It helps explain why people are motivated to act. Generally, people progress up the hierarchy. However, it is common to find an individual at varying levels of the hierarchy at different times of his life. Observing employees' needs will help you understand their self-esteem needs. Developing employees' self-esteem is vital to developing the delegating habit.

Maslow listed needs in this order, from most basic to most complex:

1. Bodily needs (food and shelter)

2. Safety (lack of danger)

3. Belonging (being part of a group)

4. Esteem (status and achievement)

5. Self-actualization (insight into one's self-growth)

Managers tend to think the lower needs are more important to their employees. Wages and job security fall into the category of bodily needs. In reality, workers say that being in on things and a sense of appreciation (esteem, belonging and self-actualization) are the most important to them. As a delegator, consider the needs of your staff members in regard to their motivation to accept your request. Consider the vast difference in these two requests:

1. "The Board of Directors has ordered another regional collection analysis. I'm sorry, but you'll have to contact each county chairperson to collect their totals and compile the various regional totals ... by tomorrow."

2. "The Board is really enthused about the campaign totals to date. They are really interested in analyzing our progress by region. We need to have updated regional totals to distribute at the meeting tomorrow."

The first delegation request motivates but does so only through fear of reprimand with an implied sense of failure. Instead, the second request accomplishes motivation with an appeal to a sense of accomplishment and belonging to the group.

A thoughtful analysis of employee motivation and work style will greatly assist you in successfully delegating. Communicating clearly and in a positive way is also essential.

Ways to Enhance Employees' Self-Esteem

- Actively listen.

- Write down others' ideas.

- Accept others' opinions.

- Take ideas seriously.

- Accept differences in others.

- Give tangible rewards.

- Give the "OK" signal when you agree with others.

- Praise the specific task.

- Say "You are right."

- Support others' actions.

- Recognize feelings.

- Give special assignments.

- Ask for help.

Communication

While communication appears to be simply a matter of voicing what you want while the other person listens, it is much more complicated than that. Each message must be encoded and decoded based on the words said, the attitude or tone projected and on other nonverbal cues subject to interpretation. A "simple" two-way communication is not simple at all. And one as complex as the delegation of work is ripe for miscommunication or misunderstanding.

Research indicates that we:

- hear half of what is said

- listen to half of what we hear

- understand only half of that

- believe half of what we understand

- remember half of what we believe

Translated into an eight-hour workday, that means you:

- spend about four hours listening

- hear about two hours' worth

- actually listen for one hour

- understand for about 30 minutes

- believe only 15 minutes' worth of information

- remember just under eight minutes' worth

The skill with which we communicate is integral to the success of the delegation process … and to all skill development areas.

Keys to Success in Developing Your People

- Be secure within yourself and comfortable in your leadership role.

- Acknowledge that the only person you can change is yourself. With others, you can only lead, assist, motivate and inspire.

- Create an environment that encourages risk and tolerates errors.

- Do whatever it takes to make sure information flows freely in all directions.

- LISTEN to and utilize input from all sources. You'll be amazed at what you will learn.

- Adjust your style to meet the individual needs of those you are endeavoring to develop.

- Set expectations high — for yourself and others.

- Be accessible and provide ample support.

- Recognize that sometimes leading means fading into the background and allowing others to take the lead ... and to get the credit.

- Remember — everyone is watching. Be a sterling role model.

Motivation Assessment Worksheet

Complete the following series of exercises to see how well you understand your employees and what motivates them … and how your employees compare to others in the work force.

Step 1: Complete this worksheet yourself. Keep your responses confidential until after your subordinates have completed a similar one in Step 2.

Rate the most important item 1, the second most important item 2 and so on, for each column:

	What Subordinates Want	What You Want
Interesting work	_____	_____
Job security	_____	_____
Full appreciation of work done	_____	_____
Personal loyalty of supervisor	_____	_____
High salary or wages	_____	_____
Tactful discipline	_____	_____
Feeling of being "in on things"	_____	_____
Promotion in the company	_____	_____
Good working conditions	_____	_____
Help with personal problems	_____	_____

Reflections

Step 2: Ask each of your subordinates to complete the exercise below without consulting one other. Arrange for input to be anonymous if you feel that would produce more direct information.

For each column, rate the most important item 1, the second most important item 2 and so on.

	What Subordinates Want	What You Want
Interesting work	_____	_____
Job security	_____	_____
Full appreciation of work done	_____	_____
Personal loyalty of supervisor	_____	_____
High salary or wages	_____	_____
Tactful discipline	_____	_____
Feeling of being "in on things"	_____	_____
Promotion in the company	_____	_____
Good working conditions	_____	_____
Help with personal problems	_____	_____

Reflections

Step 3: Compare the responses generated in Step 1 and Step 2. Then compare them to the study results presented below. How can you use these results to develop stronger working relationships with your people?

Study Results: What Workers Want

	How Subordinates Rated These Items	How Managers Think Subordinates Rated Them
Full appreciation of work done	1	8
Feeling of being "in on things"	2	10
Help with personal problems	3	9
Job security	4	2
High salary or wages	5	1
Interesting work	6	5
Promotion in the company	7	3
Personal loyalty of supervisor	8	6
Good working conditions	9	4
Tactful discipline	10	7

Reflections

10 THE DELEGATION CONFERENCE

"It is never a sign of weakness when a man in a high position delegates authority; on the contrary, it is a sign of his strength and of his capacity to deserve greatness."

— Walter Lippmann

In most organizations, delegation is a haphazard process. A conversation or note between two individuals leads to an "assignment." Chances are the communication does not include the proper information to be effective. Exploring how to effectively plan and execute a successful delegation conference is the goal of this chapter.

Why a Delegation Conference?

Effective delegation requires that the communication be carefully thought out based on the complexity and importance of the job. That communication should then take place in a planned delegation conference so the person taking on the task has all the information necessary to act and make decisions that will lead to success.

Don't delegate on the run. A hallway or noisy meeting is not the place to pass along the information required for an important delegation. Schedule sufficient time (without interruption) in your office for the delegation conference. You may want to allow 10 percent more time than your initial estimate. This will allow adequate time for discussion and questions.

The first step in delegation is preplanning on your part. You must give some thought to the delegation process prior to the actual conference. Know what supplies, resources and authority will be needed to do the work. Anticipate what questions or problems the employee might have. Commit your goals for the work to paper. Once you are ready for the delegation conference, it is helpful to remember the specific steps in the act of delegating work to someone.

The Steps in the Delegation Process

1. **State the desired results.** Explain the results that you want the person to achieve. Don't start with the actual tasks required to do the work. Start with the results you want achieved. Don't stress methods over results. You may be surprised at your employee's creativity in devising ways to achieve the desired results. The goal is mutual agreement on an objective achievement.

   Consider the difference in these two delegations:

   a) "Katie, make 500 copies of these personnel changes on company letterhead, and send one to every store manager. Get on it right away."

   b) "Katie, there are 500 store managers in the chain, and I need to let all of them know about the personnel changes as soon as possible. I'd like you to handle it. Would you give it some thought and discuss it with me in half an hour?"

   Katie may surprise you by suggesting inclusion of the memo in the avidly read company newsletter, which is about to go to press. Or she may say that the only way to do it is to send out 500 form letters. She may also surprise you by not having the vaguest idea of what to do. Great! You now have the chance to teach Katie two things: (1) that there are several ways to disseminate information to 500 people and (2) that you rely on her ideas as well as her help and will continue to ask for both as you delegate.

Having mutually agreed upon the goals of the project, commit the revised goals to paper. Remember, clearly state the goal of a project and the performance standard that will measure it in 250 words or less — one sheet of paper. If it takes longer than this, then rethink the delegation and break it down into smaller, more specific functions. Train your subordinates and recognize when there is a difference between what you want to happen and what is actually happening. Reviewing the mutually agreed-upon goals will avoid this. It minimizes confusion on all parts.

2. **Establish a timeline.** If the delegatee has a problem with your suggested deadline, be flexible when possible and work out a more suitable time limit. Allowing the subordinate to set her own deadline is preferable to forcing yours upon her. However, circumstances may sometimes dictate this. Be certain that you clearly prioritize your delegation to the employee. Realize that not everything you delegate can take precedence. This does nothing except frustrate. Do you really want her to drop everything and take on this project? Specific deadlines are a must. Avoid indefinite deadlines such as "whenever you can get to it" or "by sometime next month." Be sure to establish some kind of reporting process so that you can keep abreast of the subordinate's progress. Together, schedule the necessary checkpoint meetings. Doing this together gives the employee a chance to consider other workload demands on her time. For a simple task, one or two checkpoints may be sufficient; more complex tasks require regular meetings with specific agendas and mini-deadlines. Make sure the subordinate knows that all checkpoints and the final deadline are firm.

3. **Grant the necessary authority.** Whenever you assign work, it's vital to give the person power to act, to exercise initiative. Make sure that all persons affected by the delegation know that you've delegated authority to this person. If appropriate, introduce your subordinate to everyone involved in completing the task:

supervisors, co-workers and support staff. Make it clear that your subordinate now has the authority to do the job and that you expect her to work through any problems that arise.

4. **Assign responsibility/accountability.** Always delegate an entire task. This heightens your subordinate's interest and sense of accomplishment. Granting authority makes your delegation more effective. Make the delegation stick. Emphasize your confidence in the employee at every opportunity, even if you have to force yourself. Don't show fake confidence, but do compliment the employee throughout the task when something is done well. Your support often means more than your specific advice. Review work only at scheduled checkpoints or when the job is finished.

   Stressing the delegatee's accountability for the task accomplishes two things. First, it makes clear that "the ball is in her court." She carries the burden for results. Of course, you're still ultimately responsible to your boss, but your subordinate is accountable to you. There must be no room for confusion about that. Second, accountability contributes to the person's sense of independence. It provides positive pressure and motivation. Emphasize that the delegatee is free to make decisions relevant to this task. To some subordinates, this may be a new experience. Make it clear that, within certain limits, what they decide in this matter goes.

5. **Obtain acceptance of the project.** Always elicit from your subordinate a clear and definite acceptance of the delegated task and the intended results. You want more than murmured approval or tacit acceptance. You need an outright statement that the person agrees on the goals and the deadline. Perhaps you should both sign your copies of the revised statement of goals and timelines. Also consider the handshake as a final acceptance of the project. Although we often forget about the handshake, the axiom still applies that a person's handshake is her word. This is entirely appropriate as a way of cementing the project.

Win-Win Delegation Agreements

- **Desired results:** Identify what is to be done and when (not how).

- **Guidelines:** Specify parameters (principles, policies, etc.).

- **Resources:** Decide what human, financial, technical or organizational support is available.

- **Accountability:** Specify standards of performance and time of evaluation.

- **Consequences:** Specify — good, bad, natural and logical — what does and will happen as a result of the evaluation.

Delegation is a definite process. As you develop your delegation skills through practice, be careful to constantly review these specific steps; they will eventually become second nature to you. However, the operative word here is practice — practice, practice, practice.

Integral to the success of the delegation conference is taking time to explain the importance of the task you're delegating … and how it relates to the organization's goals. Here's why:

- It reminds individuals of the organization's goals and strengthens their importance.

- It shows that you are goal-oriented and want your subordinates to be the same.

- It helps keep the focus on high-priority matters.

- It serves as a reminder to identify activities that aren't important and to eliminate them.

- It forces you to make sure you understand and can clearly communicate your organization's goals.

Think about the last task you delegated. Describe it in a few words and then answer the following questions.

Task/Activity: _____

_____

Where did the actual act of delegation take place: your office, hallway, cafeteria or subordinate's office?

_____

_____

	Yes	No
Did you clearly define what results you wanted?		
Did you avoid telling the delegatee how to achieve the results?		
Did you establish a definite deadline for accomplishing the task?		
Did you set any intermediate reviews to monitor progress?		
Did you give the delegatee the authority necessary for success?		
Did you set clear limits to the delegated authority?		
Did you make it clear that the delegatee would be held accountable for achieving the results?		
Did you obtain her acceptance of the project and commitment to achieve the results?		
Did you solicit her ideas, comments, suggestions and questions?		
Were you satisfied when you left the meeting that she had the necessary information and authority to proceed with the task?		

Reflections

Now that you have completed your assessment, ask the delegatee to complete the following, then compare your perceptions of this delegation event.

	Yes	No
Would you describe the meeting as truly a "delegation conference"?		
Did (or will) the delegated task contribute to your development?		
Did your manager clearly define the desired results?		
Did your manager avoid telling you how to achieve the results?		
Did your manager establish a definite deadline for accomplishing the task?		
Did your manager set any intermediate reviews to monitor progress?		
Did your manager give you the authority necessary for success?		
Did your manager set clear limits to your delegated authority?		
Did your manager make it clear that you would be held accountable for achieving the results?		
Did your manager obtain your acceptance of the project and commitment to achieve the results?		
Did your manager solicit your ideas, comments, suggestions and questions?		
Were you satisfied when you left the meeting that you had the necessary information and authority to proceed with the task?		

Reflections

11 LETTING GO

"If you ride a horse, sit close and tight. If you ride a man, sit easy and light."

— Benjamin Franklin

Delegation, like a kite, will fail to fly unless given enough slack to soar. If you take back or short-circuit assignments, your interference will only frustrate subordinates. In this chapter, we'll explore what management guru Stephen Covey calls "stewardship" delegation — letting go of the process — and the personalities who find this so difficult.

"Stewardship" Delegation

Stephen Covey, author of the famed *Seven Habits of Highly Effective People* and many subsequent books, discussed two types of delegation: "Gofer" delegation and "Stewardship" delegation.

"Gofer" delegation is just that — go for this, go for that. It's the manager specifying each step one at a time. It's micromanaging the project. The boss remains intimately involved with the details, is focused on methods and process and calls the shots throughout. "Gofer" delegation is really not delegation at all.

Gofer Delegation

> Level 1 — Stand by for instruction.

> Level 2 — Investigate, provide information on possible action and wait for instruction.

Intermediate

> Level 3 — Investigate, provide information and recommend specific action. Wait for approval.

> Level 4 — Investigate, take appropriate action and provide frequent and immediate feedback.

Stewardship Delegation

> Level 5 — Investigate, take appropriate action and provide planned, periodic feedback.

"Stewardship" delegation follows the five steps detailed in Chapter 10.

- Focuses on desired results — not process

- Provides guidelines by specifying parameters and identifying known failure paths

- Identifies resources available

- Specifies accountability and standards of performance

- Identifies consequences

"Stewardship" delegation involves clear, upfront understanding and commitment regarding expectations in all five areas. It requires more time initially, then requires the delegator to let go of the project and allow the delegatee to handle it. This does not mean just forgetting about it until the deadline. Planned, consistent follow-up as detailed in Chapter 13 is essential, but the day-to-day operations and decisions are left exclusively to the delegatee.

This type of delegation is difficult for many managers. It's hard to let go of a project for which you still have ultimate responsibility (see Chapter 12). And it's sometimes a fine line between following up and interfering, especially for some specific personalities:

- Personal Producer

- Keeper of the Status Quo

- Workaholic

- Control Freak

Personal Producer: If you were a top personal producer before entering the management ranks, you may well find it difficult to step back and allow others to do the work. The tendency is to jump back into the trenches and produce! Here are four things you must do:

- Acknowledge your own limits. Any one person, no matter how good, can only do so much.

- Delegate one task at a time. If letting go is a BIG problem for you, start with one small project, then proceed to more and larger tasks. Allow yourself to get more comfortable one step at a time.

- Never again say, "I'll just do it myself." That is no longer an option. Those days are over. Do not allow yourself to take on new projects that should be delegated.

- Reassess your priorities. Do you want to be a manager or a producer? If you want to be a manager, you must learn to delegate effectively, and that means letting go.

Keeper of the Status Quo: Change is not easy for you. The unknown is dark and frightening ... not that you would admit that to anyone. You don't let others see this fear. You work very hard at keeping the potential for the unforeseen to an absolute minimum — far beyond what is necessary for prudent business practices. Try these three suggestions to help you loosen up and let go.

- Ask yourself, "What is the worst that can happen?" Then ask, "Can I handle that?" Chances are the worst-case scenario is not all that bad, once you really think about it. And if you can handle the worst (which is not likely to happen anyway), you can handle any potential outcome.

- Make small changes first. Force yourself to take small risks, then as your confidence grows, make bolder moves.

- Ask your subordinates for input. Solicit their ideas and explore the possibilities.

Workaholic: Work is your life. You're the first one in and the last one out every day. You are so driven and focused that it is hard for you to understand those who are not. As a result, you find yourself meddling and micro-managing the work of your subordinates. Try to:

- Limit your work hours. If you are working until 8 p.m. every night, make yourself leave at 7:30 p.m. every day next week. Move to 7 p.m. the following week and so on until you are working a more reasonable and normal schedule. You'll be amazed to find how much more efficient you will be — and how much easier it is to let go of some things — when time is more limited. Keep in mind: Work expands to fill the time allowed.

- Sharpen your time-management skills. Get a book. Attend a seminar. Select three or four ideas and implement them.

- Get a life. Develop an interest in something outside of work. If you can't think of anything, try skydiving.

- Lighten up on other people and recognize that sometimes "okay" really is good enough. Workaholics also tend to be perfectionists and will devote (and demand of others) incredible effort and time trying to move a task from "a really good" job to a superb one. Chances are you expect (consciously or subconsciously) your subordinates to be as committed to perfection as you are. This pursuit of perfection is dangerous. By pushing your people beyond their limits, you are decreasing productivity and destroying morale. Setting the standards unrealistically high will hurt rather than help work quality.

Control Freak: You have a profound need to be in charge, to be in control. Micromanager is your middle name. Chances are you have some of the characteristics of all the other personality types who have difficulty letting go. You think you're being helpful to your people when, in fact, you may be making them crazy.

- Force yourself to delegate — stewardship delegation, not gofer. Set up regular sessions for updating. Make them often enough that you'll be able to keep from meddling in between.

- Create the distinction between power and control. Power is the ability to make things happen by either skill or authority. Control, on the other hand, is a means of restraining, limiting or restricting something. When you have power, you don't need control.

- Implement each of the suggestions made for all the personality types presented in this chapter. They all apply to you as well.

- Recognize that it's okay to let someone or something fail. Making mistakes is part of the learning curve. Sometimes allowing someone to fail is the only way to ultimately improve his performance. Helping a delegatee grow and improve through devising a series of successes does not mean seeking to avoid all mistakes when you delegate. Not every delegated task will be done correctly. In fact, mistakes are an essential part of learning through experience. Mistakes aptly illustrate what not to do. And the person who has learned what not to do is wiser than the person who has never been allowed to venture far enough to make an error. Of course, you don't want your subordinates to make so many errors that they are intimidated by them, so limit their chances for mistakes.

Let your delegatees have an honest, fair try at it. Don't meddle! Let them do it their way, even if it's not "the right way." Avoid trespassing on authority once it is given. Make sure the jobs you give your people are whole and important and that you really give them the jobs.

Remember a subordinate's failure may simply mean that you're delegating without following through. Your controls may have failed. If a person doesn't complete a task, return to goal-setting. This is a training problem. If a person won't do something, you, as manager, need to reprimand. Proper systems for monitoring subordinates' work will prevent large-scale failures.

Once subordinates recognize that they have made errors, don't rub it in. Emphasize the positive. Find something they did right and compliment them, then correct and demonstrate how their errors might have been avoided. Remember, only reprimand when the person can do better. When you leave your people after a reprimand, you want them to think about what they did wrong, not the way you treated them. Allow yourself only a few minutes to share your feelings. When it's over, it's over. Don't keep beating on the person for the same mistake. In the same way, focus on efforts, not circumstances. When you end a reprimand with a praise, people think about their behavior, not yours. People can take only a limited amount of criticism at any one time. When they reach their limit, they become defensive, begin to reject the validity of the criticism and "tune out" altogether. So, when a subordinate really bungles an assignment, try to help him iron out the wrinkles piecemeal rather than dumping all the bad news at one time. And, mix in a little praise with the bitter medicine to help the person swallow it.

Meddle, no; ride hard, yes. Never forget: What you were responsible for before delegating you are responsible for after delegating. Follow-up is essential to the delegation process. Finding the right degree of follow-up — to guide without interfering, to protect against disaster without pampering and to advise without diminishing accountability — is a complicated, subtle aspect of the art of delegation.

1. How easy is it for you to let go of a delegated project?

2. Are you a "gofer" delegator or a "stewardship" delegator?

3. Review those projects you have had difficulty staying out of. Is there a common thread among them?

4. Create a feedback form for your subordinates to complete regarding your ongoing input on and support of their tasks. You may be surprised to learn that some of your supportive endeavors are viewed as interference.

5. What steps do you need to take to improve your stewardship delegation skills?

Reflections

12 RESPONSIBILITY

"Everybody threw the blame on me. I have noticed that they nearly always do. I suppose it is because they think I shall be able to bear it best."

— Winston Churchill

Courage is required to risk delegating. William Newman comments that executives typically have a "temperamental aversion to taking chances." Delegation is a calculated risk, he points out. We must expect that, over time, the gains will offset the losses. We must see the risk and adjust emotionally as well as intellectually in order to delegate effectively. What you were responsible for before delegating you are responsible for after delegating. And just as you are still accountable to your supervisor, you must impress upon your delegatee her responsibility and accountability in completing this assignment. This chain of responsibility is the central theme of this chapter.

It is a myth that, by delegating, the manager can avoid responsibility and consequent worry. Managers who delegate need to have broad shoulders. They must be prepared to accept the complete responsibility if their delegation is less than successful. Assigning duties to others is not a passport to freedom from worry and responsibility. That escape hatch is abdication, not delegation.

Ultimate accountability rests permanently with the person at the top. Problems inherent in delegation are tied directly to the emotions of those involved. The lunch-snatcher and the briefcase-lugger who refuse to delegate suffer from a loss-of-control feeling whenever they delegate. The delegator must think through how she will act if she discovers that things have not gone as they should. She must realize that the actions taken by others may not be the same as those she would have taken. Accommodation of differences is perhaps the hardest part of learning to delegate. While it is easy to accept the idea that people are not the same, it is much harder to accept its application.

There can be immense variations not only in the quality and quantity of work performed, but also in the ways the work is performed. The manager must be prepared to accept and live with her subordinates' methods and decisions. It's a very big order, but you cannot reap the benefits of delegation unless you are willing to accept the risks. Though you don't have to agree with your subordinates at all times, you must never leave them "hanging out to dry." Your people depend on you. Failure to support them when they need you will always undermine their trust in your leadership.

Give your subordinates credit for their successes with delegated tasks. Why should your subordinates knock themselves out if you are going to bask in the glory of their work? Teamwork is essential, but the coach has to credit her players who perform, not polish her own star. The delegator does need broad shoulders, but also a small enough ego to leave the spotlight solely for the person who did the work.

But if the project fails, you must hold the delegatee accountable, yet take the blame yourself with higher management. Sound unfair? It is. But it's an important and necessary rule to follow when delegating. The key word is trust. To build a team, your people must be able to trust that you will always be there for them.

Ten Tips When Employee Accountability Is Lacking

1. Identify the lack of accountability — specifically.

2. Determine what's causing the problem.

3. Ask the employee how she plans to solve the problem. Press her for a definitive solution, not just promises.

4. Spell out consequences so both parties know exactly what will occur if certain things do or don't happen.

5. Install hourly or daily reporting — even if it seems remedial. Slowly space out reporting times as performance improves.

6. Determine if the employee is bored or has outgrown the job. Is an alternative placement possible?

7. Show employees *how* to be accountable. Don't assume they already know.

8. Identify and remove obstacles in their path (missing tools, insufficient structure, etc.).

9. Make the employee accountable for someone else also.

10. Monitor and reward effort and progress. Acknowledge movement in the right direction, even if full accountability is not yet achieved.

1. Assess each of your delegatees in terms of general acceptance of accountability and responsibility. Next, review the "Things to Do When Accountability Is Lacking" information on pages 86-87, and outline a plan to implement each one with each employee. Specify a timetable for yourself and specific projects and problem areas to be addressed.

2. Look back over the past three to six months. List each project or task, the person or people responsible for it and its degree of success or failure. Assess your behavior upon completion. If the project was a success, did you give your people the credit with your management or take it for yourself? (1 = total credit given; 5 = total credit taken). If the project was a failure or had significant problems, did you accept the blame yourself (from higher management) or point to the individual employees involved? (1 = total acceptance of blame; 5 = total fingering of employees).

Project/Task	Person/People	Success or Failure 1 2 3 4 5 6 7 8 9 10	Credit Given Total None 1 2 3 4 5	Blame Accepted Total None 1 2 3 4 5

Reflections

3. Provide your employees with the same list of projects, and ask them to rate their success/failure and to rate you on credit given vs. blame accepted.

4. Identify your potential contributing factors to your employees' lack of accountability.
(On a scale of 1 to 5, 1 = not an issue; 5 = a major contributing factor.)

Contributing Factor	Rating 1 (Not an Issue) - 5 (Major Contributor)
1. Inadequate standards	
2. Insufficient training	
3. Conflicting objectives	
4. Failure on your part to walk the talk, to lead by example (lack of personal self-discipline)	
5. Tolerating lackluster performance and/or annoying behaviors	
6. Sharing your weaknesses	
7. Intolerance of failure	
8. Dishonesty	
9. Ignoring problems while they are small, then being forced to address them when they're huge	

Reflections

13 THE IMPORTANCE OF SPOT-CHECKING DELEGATION

"No man can see all with his own eyes or do all with his own hands. Whoever is engaged in multiplicity of business must transact much by substitution and leave some things to hazard, and he who attempts to do all will waste his life doing little."

— Samuel Johnson

While stewardship delegation is the goal — relinquishing control and authority for project completion — follow-up is essential to keep things on track. Progress reports are essential in delegation. The degree and kind of spot-checks will vary with the jobs. This chapter focuses on the importance of and tools for effective follow-up.

Case Study

Wayne, the production manager of Smith Shelving, believes in delegating authority just as the management books tell him to. A very busy man, he wants desperately to unload some responsibility on his employees. The following describes what happened on the Lacey job, a job that had to be redone because an employee made a mistake on the press dimensions. Lacey, the contractor, had been furious at the delay and had threatened to stop doing business with Smith unless the job was redone within weeks. Wayne knew it was a tight schedule when he promised Ed, the company's vice president, that he would meet it. Wayne immediately wrote out the new work order, checked all the dimensions and personally dropped it into Carl's work-order box with a big note written in red, stating, "Carl, get to this right away. Highest priority!" How was he to know that Carl, his best carpenter, would catch a cold and be out for a week? Two weeks later, when Wayne was on his way to a project status meeting, he saw Carl and asked how the job was coming. Wayne sensed trouble when Carl asked, "Which job?" When he explained which job, Carl answered, "Oh, that one. I didn't see your note until four days ago when I returned from being sick. By the way, there are a few things I wanted to get straight before I start. I guess you know we're out of those special cedar panels. How much do you want me to order? They take a week or two to deliver." Wayne was angry with Carl and berated him on the shop floor in front of others, which he knew he shouldn't have done. The pity was that Wayne was more angry at himself for not having had the good sense to check the job's progress sooner.

That's what happens to people who hope for the best and don't get it. Don't let it happen to you. Determine exactly what type of follow-up is necessary for each assignment. Obviously, a small delegation will be handled just fine with an oral report at a predetermined time and date. However, handling a major order for an irritated customer with a customer-imposed deadline may require daily progress reports. Preparation of a major funding request that you will be working on for weeks may need to have three or four written reports to follow up on progress of the project.

There are a variety of means that you can use to monitor the delegation: oral conferences, written summaries, formal reports, flow charts, checklists and calendars. The key factor here is that you must have a timeline. You must implement controls to avoid disaster. The responsibility rests with you.

Tools for Delegation

There are numerous tools available for tracking the progress of delegated projects. Elaborate software programs are available for those who need to track detailed and frequently changing data on intricate and complex projects. PERT and GANTT charts can also be used (see *Prioritize, Organize: The Art of Getting It Done* for information on these tools). For most, however, much simpler approaches are equally effective. Choose any one or a combination:

- Projects List

- Eight-Minute Meeting

- Tickler File

- Briefing Board

- Next-Steps List

- Waiting-For List

Projects List: This is a comprehensive listing of all the projects pending, assignments, progress notes and deadlines. The format is not critical; ease of use is. You might start with something such as this and then modify it to meet your individual needs and circumstances.

Project	Person Responsible	Progress Report #1	Progress Report #2	Due Date	Comments

Eight-Minute Meeting: You may decide to establish a regular face-to-face meeting. The frequency of these meetings should allow you to maintain contact often enough to have a clear sense of progress, priorities and potential problems.

Why eight minutes? Why not five … or 10? Eight is typically about the time needed to cover what needs to be done in this meeting. The problem with lengths like "five minutes" or "10 minutes" is that people tend to think of these time frames in very general terms. A length like eight minutes implies a specific amount of time. It commands respect and indicates that the communication needs to be straightforward and to the point.

Tickler Files: Also known as a follow-up file, this system is based on visual "tickler" words or numbers reminding you to take action on a task. These files could consist of 31 daily files marked 1 through 31, and/or 12 monthly files labeled with the months of the year. An accordian file placed in clear view could be used to implement the tickler system.

Oct	Nov	Dec	Next Yr	
May	Jun	Jul	Aug	Sep
31	Jan	Feb	Mar	Apr
26	27	28	29	30
21	22	23	24	25
16	17	18	19	20
11	12	13	14	15
6	7	8	9	10
1	2	3	4	5

To use a Tickler File, the files must be constantly rotated and moved. If today is August 6, the front file would be "7"; the succeeding daily files would be the remaining days of that month (8-31). Behind the "31" file would be the monthly file for the following month (September), and behind it would be the rest of the daily files (1-6). The remaining monthly files (October-August) would be placed behind these daily files.

Using the Tickler File is simple. Let's use the August 6 date as our example. If you need to follow up on Project A on *August* 15, make a note of the project, person and information to be updated, and place it in the *#15* folder. If the follow-up is for *September* 15, place a "15" in the upper right-hand corner, and put it in the *"September"* folder.

At the end of each day, pull out the next day's Tickler File (it should be in the front) and review what progress reports/meetings are scheduled for the next day. Place the now empty daily file in the back, behind the rest of the days. When the first day of a new month arrives, take out that month's folder (which will now be in front). Collate all the items into the daily files based on the dates you noted in the upper right-hand corner. Before making the distribution, however, clip together any daily files which fall on a weekend or represent a day you will not be in the office. That way, nothing can fall between the cracks.

Briefing Board: This method is a very simple tracking mechanism mounted on a wall for quick, easy and frequent visibility. This is what a Briefing Board looks like.

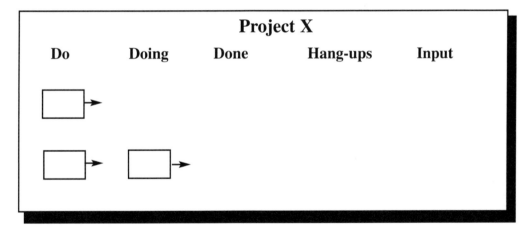

Each header ("Do, Doing, Done, Hang-ups, Input") is placed on a separate 5 x 7 card. Under "Do," post all the component tasks of the project in question. Post each on a separate 3 x 5 card so they can be moved individually and independently of the others throughout the process.

You and your subordinate can plan out the project and post each "Do" step. As you receive progress reports, move appropriate card(s) from "Do" to

"Doing." Over time, as components are completed, these cards are moved over to "Done." At a glance, you can see what's yet to be started, what's in progress and what's been finished.

Sometimes you'll find that a card stays under "Do" too long. This may indicate that there is some type of a hang-up with that step. This is a nice red flag for you to bring this situation to the attention of your subordinate so that he can address the situation. Identify what the problem is, write it on a card and post it under "Hang-ups." The "Input" column is for suggestions from you, the subordinate or anyone else who may have an idea how to get past the problem. This is a great way to get additional input without rearranging everyone's schedule to have a meeting!

You can use one Briefing Board to track multiple projects. Simply color-code the component cards for easy visual tracking, or color-code the cards according to individual responsibility: John's are blue, Jane's are yellow, etc. Be creative.

Next-Steps List: This is just what it appears to be, a list of the next steps you need to take. Let's say Jane is an outstanding worker with an excellent track record of completing assignments with little or no direct supervision. Your next-step entry for her project might simply be: "See Jane on 10/17 (next month) for an eight-minute follow-up on ABC Project."

If Sally, on the other hand, requires much closer supervision to stay on track, that entry might read: "Review with Sally on 9/26 (tomorrow) status of xyz component, discuss potential pitfalls and identify what should happen next."

The beauty of the Next-Steps List is that you can make each entry as detailed or as broad as appropriate and as near-term or long-range as necessary. Then you can clear your mind without fear of forgetting an important next step.

Waiting-For List: Here you can list all the things you are "waiting for" from your subordinates: a return call from John, an update from Sue or an analysis from John. At a glance, you can see the commitments your people have made to you regarding information you need to help them be successful.

Tips for Improving Poor Performance

- Find the history of the problem behavior. Most have one.

- Ask yourself, "Am I partly (or totally) responsible? Have I contributed to the problem in any way?"

- Read between (and behind) the lines. Don't just take words or behaviors at face value.

- Treat the employee as an adult, and expect adult behavior.

- Clarify all the issues before you confront the individual (or group).

- Gain agreement about the problem.

- Determine a course of action. Participation in the process by all the individuals involved is helpful.

- Gain agreement on the necessary course of action.

- Identify the consequences — positive and negative — and tie them to basic needs.

- Reward achievement.

Assess your follow-up skills and techniques:

1. Is your follow-up a regularly scheduled, planned routine (1) or a catch-as-catch-can series of sporadic events typically involving some type of crisis (10)?

     1   2   3   4   5   6   7   8   9   10

2. Which of the follow-up tools are you already using? How could you improve your use of them? When (exactly) will you begin using each of the remaining tools — at least on a trial basis?

Tool	Using Now? Yes	No	Improvement Ideas	Starting Date for New Tools
Projects List				
Tickler File				
Eight-Minute Meeting				
Briefing Board				
Next-Steps List				
Waiting-For List				

14 MAKING IT STICK — HANDLING REVERSE DELEGATION

"I like the sayers of 'No' better than the sayers of 'Yes'."

— Ralph Waldo Emerson

Once you've assigned a task to a subordinate, don't allow yourself to be manipulated into relieving the subordinate of the responsibility for taking the next step. If you're not careful, this can happen in the blink of an eye. Identifying ways to avoid such a situation is the central focus of this chapter.

It's appropriate to view delegated tasks and problems as monkeys. When you delegate, you pass along the ongoing responsibility for the day-to-day care and feeding of the monkey to your employee, while still maintaining ultimate responsibility for its life or death. Decisions to be made about obstacles and problems within the delegated projects are NOT your responsibility, NOT your monkey!

If you allow yourself to be buttonholed in a hallway or the elevator, the talk may be, "Boss, we've got a problem." The "we" implies that the subordinate believes that you and she are sharing the responsibility for the next step. Say the wrong thing such as, "Let me get back to you," and the "monkey" is right back on your shoulders.

Handle this kind of situation by making the next move the subordinate's. For example, say to the subordinate, "You're right. There is a problem there. Give me a call tomorrow, and tell me how it should be handled. What are the alternatives?" Avoid using the word "we" in your response.

You might even ask the employee to write out the problem in 25 words or less and to list three alternative solutions. This forces her to truly identify the core issue without wasting your time detailing all the extraneous, peripheral minutiae. It lets her develop her problem-solving skills, and it gives her a tool to deal with the monkey while leaving the monkey squarely on her back where it belongs.

Remember, the best manager isn't always the one with the best answers, but the one with the best questions. Each time you hand out an assigned task, your subordinate can act in one of five different ways:

1. Do nothing until told.

2. Ask what to do.

3. Recommend action, then take it.

4. Act, then advise you immediately.

5. Act, then report to you in a routine manner.

The astute delegator will not permit numbers one and two to occur. Do so, and you'll become so occupied with what subordinates are doing that your time will become subordinate-imposed time. You won't be able to focus on what's important to you. You're no longer in control.

Always remember that time spent in doing things for your subordinates is always subordinate-imposed time, says William Oncken, Jr., author of *Managing Management Time*. Time spent doing things with them is always discretionary time. "Whenever possible, do things with them rather than for them."

There are a variety of reasons for the phenomenon of reverse delegation:

1. **Your subordinate wishes to avoid risk.** It is easier to ask the boss than for your subordinate to decide for herself. Asking the boss is a way of sharing the responsibility.

2. **Your subordinate is afraid of criticism.** Be careful to establish a sound system of offering constructive criticism in private.

3. **Your subordinate lacks confidence.** Be patient and delegate anyway. Without experience, no one will develop confidence.

4. **Your subordinate lacks the necessary information and resources.** No responsibility should be delegated without the requisite tools and authority.

5. **The boss wants to be needed.** The manager who is insecure with delegating authority to others is easily discernible. Employees soon sense whether the manager truly wants them to act on their own. If not, they will cater to the boss's need for omnipotence.

Often, people will go back to the boss with questions, not because they truly have questions, but because they really want reassurance or praise for their efforts. Remember to catch them doing something right. Constantly compliment and reinforce when small parts of tasks are done well. Training your staff to handle delegations is a long and sometimes arduous road. Be patient, constantly review the process, and keep your guard up against reverse delegation.

It's important to redouble your commitment to empowering and motivating your employees and to eliminate behaviors on your part that contribute to the employees' insecurities or inability to handle their monkeys alone.

Ways to Empower and Motivate

1. **Encourage employees to participate actively in team and company goals and planning.** Look for every opportunity to allow all employees throughout the organization to be active participants in the decision-making process. Minimize top-down directives.

2. **Treat each person as an individual, not just as a means to an end or as a cog in a wheel.** Find appropriate times and ways to inquire about them and their families, about a big personal event or whether the roof got repaired.

3. **Acknowledge individual contributions.** Make sure they know you give them full credit all the way up the chain of command. Praise in public and correct in private.

4. **Listen, listen, listen.** When they come to you, give them your full attention. If you cannot be interrupted, immediately set up an appointment when you can focus exclusively on them and their issue.

5. **Be interested in their career development.** Meet with them and discuss their goals and their desires. Let them know you see their potential. Encourage growth. Encourage learning. Help them take on additional responsibility and be available to offer support.

6. **Be clear in your communication.** Provide information that will give both purpose to their activities and an understanding of your expectations.

7. **Back them up.** When things go wrong, take the blame yourself. The buck stops at your desk. Never tell your superiors how dreadful a job an employee has done. Tell them how you will prevent a repeat performance.

8. **Don't micromanage.** Show you have trust in your employees. Let them have the freedom to make some of the decisions as to how to do the job at hand. Allow them to make mistakes as a learning tool. Let them know that mistakes are okay and that you fully support their decisions. Provide positive reinforcement.

9. **Ask those in the trenches for suggestions of better ways to get their jobs done.** Pay attention to the answers.

10. **Let them work to their strengths.** If you feel they have weaknesses that need strengthening, have them work on those as well. Just be sure you give them ample opportunity to do those things they do well. This helps build their confidence and enhances overall performance and morale.

11. **Let your employees help you be successful.** Why are you doing it all yourself?

12. **Be a coach.** The best way to empower and motivate employees is not to manage them. It's to coach them.

Identify at least three monkeys you are carrying that should be carried by someone else.

Outline a plan to return the care and feeding of these monkeys to their rightful owners.

Assess your relationship with each of your subordinates.

Who tosses you the most monkeys?

Who handles their own with grace and ease?

What is the difference in your approach to these individuals?

What can you learn from the excellent "monkey handler" to assist you in improving the performance of your weaker workers?

What, specifically, can you do to help motivate your employees and to make them feel more empowered? Outline a plan of action.

Reflections

15 HANDLING PROJECTS DELEGATED TO YOU

"Heaven ne'er helps the men who will not act."

— Sophocles

Now that you have given thought to your delegation consciousness, what about your role as the delegatee? The chances are that in addition to being the delegator, you are also, on occasion, the delegatee. What happens when your supervisor delegates a project to you? How do you handle it? Let's explore these issues in this final chapter.

The first thing to ask when you receive a delegation is, "Why me?" What prompted the boss to delegate this job to me? Is this something that I am particularly adept at? Is this something that I really need to learn more about to be better at my job? What will my performance on this task tell my boss about my abilities? Once you determine why, it is easier to chart your activities to accomplish the task.

Be sure that you have your own agenda for the delegation conferences:

1. Do you understand what the desired results are?

2. Do you understand specifically how the results will be measured?

3. Do you agree with the time frame for the work? Can you handle this project and your other obligations at the same time?

4. Do you have the authority, resources and people to do the work?

Keep in mind the professional advantages you'll gain by accepting the delegation challenge:

1. Successful delegation will make your boss look good. Put in the extra effort to make the delegation work. This will increase the likelihood of future delegations being made to you.

2. Successful delegation will give you invaluable professional experience. Obviously, the praise you receive for successfully handling a delegation will bring your name to mind for the future projects. If you feel that you are lacking experience in a specific area of operation, explain the mutual advantages of delegation to your supervisor.

Remember, a prime motivator to your employees is your demonstration of the correct delegation behavior for them. Most of the principles that apply here are the flip side of all the concepts previously discussed in motivating your employees to accept the challenge of delegation.

A note regarding delegations directed to you: If your boss is a skilled delegator, you are lucky. If his delegation consciousness could use some improvement, this is a challenge for you. Take the opportunities that arise to discuss the advantages of him delegating projects to you. Be careful here: You must not make your boss think that you are moving in on his territory. Be aware of his sensitivities and insecurities. You must subtly point out the advantages of delegation in increasing his productivity. No manager wants to delegate his way to a demotion. In order to reinforce your manager's sense of security, remember to emphasize the following:

1. Delegation produces increased results/productivity.

2. Delegation increases efficiency.

3. Delegation requires checks and balances for control.

4. Delegation — properly executed — makes everyone look good!

1. What projects has your boss delegated to you in the past three months? How many were delegated to you personally vs. those delegated to you for completion by your group?

2. How good are your boss's delegation skills? What are his strengths? What are his areas for improvement? What specific items from this book would be helpful to your boss?

3. Review the information in Chapters 8 and 11 regarding personality types, and apply them to you and your boss. What adjustments could you make in your work style to improve the delegation process and working relationship between the two of you.

Reflections
Reflections

NOTES

INDEX

A

accountability   1-2, 4, 43, 45, 72-73, 83, 85-89
agenda for the delegation conference   105
assessing personalities of delegatees   52
assess subordinates   37-38, 41
authority   2, 5-6, 8, 13, 19-20, 40, 49, 59-60, 69, 71-72, 74-75, 81-82, 91, 101, 105
avoiding errors in goal setting   45

B

barriers   19, 21-24
   in the manager   19
   in the situation   22
   in the subordinate   21
benefits
   for subordinates   10
   for the manager   9
   to the organization   11
briefing board   93, 95-96, 98

C

communication   58, 62, 69, 94, 102

D

delegatee selection   50, 55

delegatee personalities

    one-man band   52-53

    know-it-all   52-53

    no way, jack!   52-53

    who cares, anyway?   52-53

    workhorse   52

delegate

    goals   2, 5-6, 27, 42-43, 45-47, 50-51, 69-70, 73, 91

    reasons to   15

    what not to   25, 31, 33

    what to   25, 27, 37, 39

delegating   10, 12-13, 19, 21, 23-24, 27, 31, 33-34, 37, 52-54, 57, 59-61, 70,
    73, 82-83, 85-86, 91, 101, 106

    steps to effective   5

delegation

    conference   56, 69-71, 73, 75

    gofer   77-78, 81, 84

    intermediate   74-75, 78

    musts   2

    reverse   99-101

    steps   70

    stewardship

    ten secrets of successful, effective   23

    things to remember   40

    tips   7, 97

    tools   91-92, 101

    what it is   1

desired results   70, 73, 78, 105

developing people   64
direct results   50, 55

E
eight-minute meeting   94
evaluation   3, 31, 38, 43, 45, 47, 51, 55, 73
expectations   2, 23-24, 43, 49, 52-53, 56-58, 64, 78, 102

F
five ways to reach a goal faster   46

G
goals   2, 5-6, 16, 23-24, 27, 33, 35, 43-47, 50, 58, 70-73, 101-102
gofer delegation   77-78

I
intermediate delegation   78

M
managerial ineffectiveness   1
Maslow's hierarchy of human needs   60
manager's excuses for not delegating   21
motivating employees   58
motivation assessment worksheet   65

N
next-steps list   96, 98

O
objectives   44

P

personal attributes of a successful delegator   4
personalities
    control freak   79, 81
    keeper of the status quo   79-80
    personal producer   79
    workaholic   79-80
projects list   93
Pygmalion in Management Effect   57

R

reasons managers don't delegate   22
responsibility   2, 10, 12-13, 15, 19, 21, 24, 26, 32-33, 39, 45, 54, 56-57, 59, 72, 79, 85, 87-88, 91-92, 96, 99-102
reverse delegation, reasons for   100

S

stewardship delegation   77-78, 81, 84, 91

T

ten tips when employee accountability is lacking   86
tickler files   94
timelines   47, 52, 71-72, 92
tips for improving poor performance   97
tools for delegation
    briefing board   93, 95-96, 98
    eight-minute meeting   94, 98
    next-steps list   96, 98
    projects list   93, 98
    tickler files   94, 98
    waiting-for list   93, 96, 98

W

waiting-for list   93, 96, 98
ways to empower and motivate   101
ways to enhance self-esteem   62
win-win delegation agreements   73
work style profile   39
working smarter, steps to   viii

NOTES

NOTES

NOTES

Buy any 3, get 1 FREE!

Get a 60-Minute Training Series™ Handbook FREE ($14.95 value)* when you buy any three. See back of order form for full selection of titles.

These are helpful how-to books for you, your employees and co-workers. Add to your library. Use for new-employee training, brown-bag seminars, promotion gifts and more. Choose from many popular titles on a variety of lifestyle, communication, productivity and leadership topics. Exclusively from National Press Publications.

DESKTOP HANDBOOK ORDER FORM

Ordering is easy:

1. Complete both sides of this Order Form, detach, and mail, fax or phone your order to:

   Mail: National Press Publications
   P.O. Box 419107
   Kansas City, MO 64141-6107

   Fax: 1-913-432-0824
   Phone: 1-800-258-7248
   Internet: www.natsem.com

2. Please print:

   Name_____ Position/Title _____

   Company/Organization_____

   Address_____City _____

   State/Province_____ZIP/Postal Code _____

   Telephone (____)_____ Fax (____)_____

   Your e-mail: _____

3. Easy payment:

   ❏ Enclosed is my check or money order for $_____ (total from back).
   Please make payable to National Press Publications.

   Please charge to:
   ❏ MasterCard   ❏ VISA   ❏ American Express

   Credit Card No. _____ Exp. Date_____

   Signature_____

• •

MORE WAYS TO SAVE:

SAVE 33%!!! BUY 20-50 COPIES of any title ... pay just $9.95 each ($11.25 Canadian).

SAVE 40%!!! BUY 51 COPIES OR MORE of any title ... pay just $8.95 each ($10.25 Canadian).

* $17.00 in Canada

60-MINUTE TRAINING SERIES™ HANDBOOKS

TITLE	RETAIL PRICE	QTY	TOTAL
8 Steps for Highly Effective Negotiations #424	$14.95		
Assertiveness #4422	$14.95		
Balancing Career and Family #4152	$14.95		
Common Ground #4122	$14.95		
Delegate for Results #4592	$14.95		
The Essentials of Business Writing #4310	$14.95		
Everyday Parenting Solutions #4862	$14.95		
Exceptional Customer Service #4882	$14.95		
Fear & Anger: Slay the Dragons … #4302	$14.95		
Fundamentals of Planning #4301	$14.95		
Getting Things Done #4112	$14.95		
How to Coach an Effective Team #4308	$14.95		
How to De-Junk Your Life #4306	$14.95		
How to Handle Conflict and Confrontation #4952	$14.95		
How to Manage Your Boss #493	$14.95		
How to Supervise People #4102	$14.95		
How to Work With People #4032	$14.95		
Inspire & Motivate: Performance Reviews #4232	$14.95		
Listen Up: Hear What's Really Being Said #4172	$14.95		
Motivation and Goal-Setting #4962	$14.95		
A New Attitude #4432	$14.95		
The New Dynamic Comm. Skills for Women #4309	$14.95		
The Polished Professional #4262	$14.95		
The Power of Innovative Thinking #428	$14.95		
The Power of Self-Managed Teams #4222	$14.95		
Powerful Communication Skills #4132	$14.95		
Present With Confidence #4612	$14.95		
The Secret to Developing Peak Performers #4692	$14.95		
Self-Esteem: The Power to Be Your Best #4642	$14.95		
Shortcuts to Organized Files & Records #4307	$14.95		
The Stress Management Handbook #4842	$14.95		
Supreme Teams: How to Make Teams Work #4303	$14.95		
Thriving on Change #4212	$14.95		
Women and Leadership #4632	$14.95		

Sales Tax

All purchases subject to state and local sales tax.

Questions?

Call

1-800-258-7248

Subtotal	$
Add 7% Sales Tax *(Or add appropriate state and local tax)*	$
Shipping and Handling *($3 one item; 50¢ each additional item)*	$
TOTAL	$

08/01